INSIGHT POCKET GUIDES

Costa B

Alicante & Murcia

APA PUBLICATIONS
Part of the Langenscheidt Publishing Group

Iberian Peninsula
160 km / 100 miles
Atlantic
Ocean
FRANCE
SPAIN
PORTUGAL
MOROCCO
ALGERIA
PYRENEES
CORDILLERA
CANTABRICA
SIERRA MORENA
SIERRA
NEVADA
ANDORRA
Mediterranean
Sea
ISLAS BALEARES
(BALEARIC ISLANDS)
MENORCA
MALLORCA
IBIZA
FORMENTERA
Palma
C. Ortegal
La Coruña
C. Finisterre
Lugo
Gijón
Oviedo
León
Santander
Bilbao
San
Sebastián
Bayonne
Pau
Tarbes
Toulouse
Montpellier
Nîmes
Sète
Carcassonne
Perpignan
C. Creus
Girona
Barcelona
Terrassa
Lleida
Zaragoza
Pamplona
Logroño
Burgos
Soria
Orense
Vigo
Braga
Porto
Aveiro
Benavente
Valladolid
Duero
Douro
Salamanca
Segovia
Calatayud
Ebro
Tarragona
Tortosa
Guarda
Coimbra
Castelo
Branco
Leiria
Madrid
Alcalá
de Henares
Cuenca
Teruel
Castellón
de la Plana
Toledo
Tajo
Tejo
Santarém
Lisboa
Setúbal
Cáceres
Badajoz
Evora
Beja
C. de San
Vicente
Lagos
Faro
Ciudad
Real
Guadiana
Almadén
Valdepeñas
Zafra
Córdoba
Sevilla
Huelva
Jerez de la
Frontera
Cádiz
Jaén
Guadalquivir
Granada
Málaga
Almería
C. de Gata
Águilas
Cartagena
Murcia
Elx
Alicante
C. de
la Nao
Valencia
Júcar
Albacete
Tarifa
Gibraltar
Strait
of
Gibraltar
Ceuta
(Sp.)
Tanger
Tétouan
Larache
Melilla
(Sp.)
Oran
Mostaganem
Ech
Cheliff
Algiers
Blida
Chott
El Hodna
Tlemcen
ISLAS CANARIAS
(CANARY ISLANDS)
LA PALMA
TENERIFE
Sta. Cruz
de Tenerife
GOMERA
HIERRO
GRAN
CANARIA
Las
Palmas
FUERTEVENTURA
LANZAROTE

Welcome!

The Costa Blanca is justly famous for its blue skies, white beaches and superb sports facilities. But the tourist geography of this cosmopolitan coast suggests little or nothing of what lies behind it: fertile river valleys running up between the mountains like hair-line cracks in china; historic towns clumped below their castles; Moorish terracing carved out of the hillsides; and splendid baroque architecture.

In these pages, Vicky Hayward, an Insight Guides correspondent in Spain, has devised a range of itineraries to bring you the best of this beautiful region. Seven full-day itineraries link the essential sights and 16 Pick & Mix itineraries highlight other interesting aspects of the area. Complementing the itineraries are sections on entertainment, eating out, shopping and sport, which in turn are followed by a practical information section.

Vicky Hayward lives in Madrid, working as a freelance writer. She first got to know Costa Blanca as a child on family holidays: 'One of my clearest childhood memories of Spain is of a drive south to Alicante in the early 1960s. My brother and I spent the journey leaning out of the car's windows, watching the dust billow up behind and waving at the farmers riding to the fields on their donkeys. In the first hour, our combined donkey tally reached over 200.' This journey was the start of a lasting love for a region which, though somewhat depleted in terms of donkeys these days, still retains many unique charms. This guide shows you exactly where to find them.

C O N T E N T S

History & Culture

Highlights of the Costa Blanca

Seven full-day itineraries concentrating on the area's chief pleasures and attractions.

Pages 2/3: Benimantell and the Guadalest Valley

Pick & Mix Itineraries

A further 16 itineraries, this time catering to a variety of time frames and tastes.

Pages 8/9: local specialities

Entertainment, Dining, Shopping & Sport

Calendar of Special Events

Practical Information

Maps

Cifuentes
R. Tajo
Molina de Aragón
Monreal del C.
Montalban
P. de Santolea
R. Guadalope
Encanadé
1938
Tortosa
R. Ebre
La Cava
Amposta
St. Carles de la Ràpita
Perales de Alf.
Morella
Turmell
1284
R. Servol
1246
Bienvenida
R. Guadiela
Priego
Orihuela del Trem.
SERRANIA DE CUENCA
La Iglesuela
Vinaroz
Benicarlo
Albarracin
Teruel
SRA. DE GUDAR
Albocácer
Cañaveras
MONTES UNIVERSALES
R. Turia
R. Linares
R. de la Viuda
Torreblanca
R. Júcar
Javalambre
2022
R. Mijares
Lucena del Cid
COSTA DEL AZAHAR
Naharros
Cuenca
Cañete
Torre Baja
SRA. DE ESPADAN
Castelló de la Plana
Almanzora
Santa Cruz de Moya
Viver
Nules
Burriana
Campalbo
1329
Salada
1585
Segorbe
Villares del Saz
Almodóvar del Pinar
Chelva
Pantano de Alarcón
Pantano de Generalísimo
La Almarcha
Sagunto
Liria
R. Turia
Pantano de Contreras
Motilla del Palancar
Gulf
of
Valencia
Tejo
1250
Minglanilla
Requena
València
R. Zancara
Moluengo
1040
Torrente
Palma de Mallorca
S. Clemente
R. Cabriel
R. Magro
La Albufera
R. Júcar
Villarobledo
Casas Ibáñez
Eivissa (Ibiza)
Cofrentes
La Roda
Cullera
L A
M A N C H A
Caroch
1124
Alcira
Munera
1077
C. María Cristina
Molatón
Xàtiva
(Játiva)

Costa Blanca Region

40 km / 25 miles

History &

It is often hard to give a sense of immediacy to prehistory. But in this southeastern area of Spain, the quantity and cultural sophistication of archaeological finds seem to telescope that huge span of time that so dwarfs our own. The first evidence of human settlement goes back to the Palaeolithic era, when man lived mainly on the fringes of the Cantabrian mountains and close to the eastern coast. In the range of low sierras between Alcoy and Yecla, a series of sites, not yet fully explored, track an evolution from cave dwelling, c50,000BC – later with paintings of hunting and animals, as at La Sarga, near Alcoy, and Monte Arabí, at Yecla (c6000BC) – to the walled towns of Iberian culture.

The origin of the Iberians is still obscure, but archaeologists have established that by the 6th century BC they were spread through present-day Valencia, Albacete and Murcia, living as autonomous tribes in walled towns. Two Bronze Age cultures developed alongside one another: the Argaric to the south and Valencian to the north, with their boundary along the Vinalopo valley. Both were skilled in working precious metals such as copper, silver, iron and gold. Like the much earlier cave paintings, these ornaments and jewellery show African influences and, even to the modern eye, have an almost contemporary sophistication.

Under the Iberians, the Argaric and Valencian cultures in this region merged to become the Contestani. These farming people, who kept large herds of cattle and grew wheat, were remarkably receptive to the traders who came to their shores. First came the Phoenicians, in the 8th century BC, who mined in the sierras and introduced fish-salting, the potter's wheel, the date palm, vine, fig and olive. Then, in the 5th century BC, came the Massiliot Greeks, who charted the coast and built commercial and manufacturing settlements along it. Absorbing and adapting these Mediterranean influences, the Iberians produced superb decorated ceramics and sculptures, including the serene Dama de Elche, one of a series of stone carvings thought to be linked to practices or rites involving the worship of a mother/fertility goddess.

Inevitably, with their rich mineral deposits, the Iberians were soon sucked into imperial politics. After the western Phoenician colonies dependent on Carthage lost the first Punic War – and their influence in southern Italy – they began extending their power in southern Spain, triggering Iberian resistance and then, in 218BC, Roman invasion. Under Publio Cornelio Scipio, the army moved slowly south from present-day Catalunya, nine years later conquering the Carthaginian capital Quart Hades, which the Romans renamed Cartago Nova – today Cartagena.

The coastal plain ends abruptly at the Sierra de Maigmo

Iberia would take another two centuries to be fully tamed, but the towns of this coastline, linked by the arterial highway of the Vía Agusta, flourished long before then. Here, in Hispania Citerior – later Tarraconensis – the Roman generals wintered, fish-salting factories were built along the coast, a network of roads was developed, irrigation systems were set up and large quantities of wine, olive oil and wheat were produced for export to Rome. The economic jewel remained the mines behind Cartago Nova, where, at their peak, 40,000 Iberian slaves extracted lead and silver. Great tracts of forest, chopped down to provide timber, were replaced by *esparto* grass – used to make bags for carrying coal, sandals and helmets – and the city was renamed Cartago Espartaria.

Roman colonisation slowly assimilated Iberian culture and redrew its human geography. The main towns shifted to the coast, with Cartaga, the provincial capital, standing supreme. Today its splendour is largely buried, but the ruined Catedral Vieja and necropolis retain some of the earliest surviving evidence of Christianity's general acceptance in Spain by the 4th century, after a long struggle from the bottom up. In the decline running up to the collapse of Roman power in the 5th century, many towns were either abandoned and replaced by rural settlements, or changed site, moving – like Lucentum (Alicante), for example – to more defensive positions. Initially, most of this area was controlled by the Byzantines, but by the middle of the 7th century it had fallen, like the rest of the country, to the Visigoths.

The Arab Conquest

Just as the Romans had invited the Visigoths to help them keep disorder at bay, so a dynastic Visigothic squabble opened the door to the virtually complete Muslim takeover of the peninsula in three brief years (711–14). The political history of the eight centuries of

Below: Moorish terracing, Pego. Right: collecting wild camomile

NATURAL HISTORY

Since the 1970s, the areas of Spanish coast and countryside protected or marked out for the value of their landscape and wildlife have increased enormously, highlighting their often overlooked importance and value. There are various categories: *parque natural* and *parque natural terrestre-marítimo* (the latter covering both sea and shore), which are the most stringently protected; *paraje natural*, an interesting landscape; *reserva de caza* and *reserva integral*, protecting the wild-life. These are marked on maps, although sometimes not very accurately, since certain proposals for protection haven't come to fruition due to opposition from local landowners and/or industry, and others are too new for the maps.

Along the shoreline itself, some capes and offshore islands have kept a remarkable submarine life, which flourishes on the sea grass (*Posidonia oceanica*). It used to cover the entire continental platform, but is now only left in patches. For this reason Tabarca, which still has turtles, is a marine reserve with controlled public access. Other areas that stand out are the Islote de Benidorm and the Islas Hormigas (both recently registered as marine reserves), the Cabo de la Nao, and Calblanque, protected as an *espacio natural*. There is a project pending to make the entire Mar Menor a reserve, but it remains to be seen whether this will become a reality.

The best known *parques naturales* within easy reach of the coast are the pine forests of the Sierra de Espuña (the second largest *parque* in Spain) and the wetlands of the Albufera. But there are others within Alicante province: the Peñón d'Ifach, with interesting plant life, Pico del Montgó to the south of Denia and Carrascal de Font Roja, which is an important last outpost of mixed Mediterranean woodland with *carrascas* (kermes oaks). As well as the Sierra de Espuña, Murcia region has La Valle, an area of sierras to the south of Murcia city.

The string of salt-lakes down the coast were upgraded from *parajes naturales* to *parques naturales* in 1994 and are host to much interesting bird life: flamingoes, grebes and other birds of passage. The Lagunas de la Mata and Torrevieja, and the Laguna de El Hondo have been intelligently transformed in recent years into ecological activity and education centres, and the Salinas de Santa Pola have been visited by 250 recorded species.

Besides this, there are areas of great beauty and interest with no special protection: the Barrancos del Infierno and Mascarat, the Sierras d'Aitana and de Mariola in the northern hill ranges and valleys, the Guardamar Dunes and small Murcian sierras (for example Yecla, Jumilla, de la Muela and Villafuerte) further south.

Last but not least, there are the oriental *palmerales*, or palm forests, thought to have been planted by the Phoenicians, among which Elche's municipal park and privately owned Hort del Cura are outstanding. Now that these palm trees have little commercial value other than for gardeners, there are worries that the forests, too, are a threatened and slowly disappearing part of the landscape.

Muslim presence which followed is complex, with many local twists and turns. Tribes and dynasties from various parts of the Arab world – in this sense the name Moors, used as a convenient umbrella for the Muslims, is strictly speaking inaccurate – invaded and ruled in succession, while the power structure shifted from an all-powerful caliphate, set up in Cordoba in the 8th century, to *taifas*, or splinter kingdoms of the 11th century, then to territorial control by the Almoravids and Almohads, Berber tribes from Morocco's Atlas mountains who invaded in the 12th century. One of the most curious twists to the tale is the story of Teodomiro, Visigothic ruler of Orihuela, who ingeniously tricked the invading Muslim forces by arming the city walls with women and children dressed in men's clothing – or so legend has it – and, on this basis, managed to negotiate his control of a *kura*, or semi-sovereign state, which stretched from Lorca in the south to Alicante city in the north (713–821). As a result, most of this area remained more Visigothic than Muslim until the 10th century.

Water wheel at La Ñora

But the long-term impact of the Moors' colonisation is hard to overestimate in this region. For while its religious and political institutions were swept away after the reconquest, its imprint has remained on every other area of life. This is frequently pointed out to the visitor: in everyday details of architecture – horseshoe arches, entrance porches (*zaguanes*), 18th-century stuccoes, ceramic tiles (*azulejos*) and a general flair for decorative detail; in the survival of Arab placenames; in the Middle Eastern influence in local dishes; and in music, dances and fiestas.

Most important of all, however, was the transformation of the landscape through Moorish circular irrigation techniques, which were linked to the symbolic importance of water in Islam. Their water wheels and irrigation channels in the river valleys allowed the widespread cultivation of oranges, lemons, almonds and rice, which still forms the basis of the region's agricultural economy today. Equally, under the *taifas*, the flowering of urban culture and craft workshops – paper manufacture and silk making, boat building and ceramics – was

Lorca Castle

to provide the basis of the medieval urban economy and, much later on, the region's first industries.

Alongside this, the regional map was redrawn again, fragmenting the Visigoths' tentative national political unity. Rural hamlets or *quaryas*, called *alquerías* by the Spanish, were protected and controlled by a network of *husum,* or castles, and laid down in a pattern which has remained to this day in the Ricote and Gallinera valleys. Murcia city, founded only in the 9th century, acquired power as the head of a *taifa* stretching north to include Alicante town, and even became the capital of al-Andalus briefly in the 13th century; Denia, the second city of the region and capital of another *taifa*, grew to a population of around 50,000 and was an important cultural centre. Orihuela and Alcoy – both with a large number of cloth and dye workshops – Játiva, Cocentaina and Lorca won new commercial and administrative strength as well.

The Reconquest

When the Reconquest finally arrived here in the 13th century, it moved swiftly southwards in a two-pronged drive by Castile and Aragon, more often taking the form of local surrender pacts than military victories. At the same time, the treaties carving up the new territories moved the Aragonese boundary significantly south over the course of the century. In the end it was the Treaty of Torrellas, made in 1304, which more or less fixed the border for the next five centuries, dividing the old kingdom of Murcia in half, with Orihuela and the lower Segura valley passing to Aragon and the rump remaining for Castile.

As social history, the Reconquest was a much slower process, with resettlement continuing in uneven spurts up until the 18th century. There were various specific reasons for this, among them Muslim rebellions, the stultifying effect of the nearby frontier zone with Moorish Granada – the final Cortes to raise money and arms was held at Orihuela in 1488 – and the expulsion of the dynamic Jewish community in 1492. On top of this there were the inevitable general problems of kick-starting economic growth against the background of repeated flooding and droughts, outbursts of plague and continued warring between Castile and Aragon.

However, most large towns had begun to take on less defensive profiles by the end of the 14th century. Their separate Muslim and

Christian quarters typically spilled down and away from the protection of the castle above (Cocentaina is the clearest surviving example of this layout, with the Raval and Villa still quite distinct). Churches, often on the sites of 'purified' mosques, usually took more than several centuries to build for lack of funds, with spacious late Gothic elements (and clear Catalan influences in Aragonese territory) overlaid by trimmings in florid late Isabelline Gothic and 16th-century Plateresque. Santa María in Alicante and the Cathedral at Orihuela are good examples of this blend. In the countryside, vineyards were planted to supply the new demand for wine.

The palaces and castles reflected another aspect of social structure: the growing division of the reconquered territories into señorial power blocks. The Marquesado de Villena, virtually a state-within-a-state owing allegiance to Castile, was the most powerful of these, but huge tracts of land were granted to other noble families too over the course of time: Onil, Ibi, Castalla and Albatera went to the Marqueses de las Dos Aguas from Valencia; Cocentaina, Callosa and Benidorm to the de Laurias from Catalunya; great chunks of Murcia to the Marquéses of Velez. Likewise, the southern frontier towns around the Sierra de Espuña were for centuries governed by the Orders of the Knights Templar and Santiago, who had helped Alfonso X of Castile to victory in his campaign to conquer Murcia. In the end, the privileges of these and many other, often absentee, landlords came to be bitterly resented.

It was well after the union of Castile and Aragon through the marriage of Isabella and Ferdinand (1474) that the nobility began to cooperate with the Church and state. At the same time, since the two kingdoms continued to be governed under separate systems – the Aragonese respecting the local laws of its various kingdoms while the Castilian merged regions under a centralised system – the political dividing line between them hardened and became linguistic (*valenciano* to the north and west and *castellano* to the south and east), social and economic. Aragon's trades – cloth, metalwork, leather, furniture making and boat building – grew out of resourcefulness rather than primary materials; in Murcia, the silk industry and mines were thriving again, but the mainstay of the economy, agriculture, was held back by aridity.

For all their differences, the two areas shared many of the same problems. One was continued outbursts of plague, which led to a marked drop in population in the 17th century. Another was Berber piracy which, against the background of Islamic expansion under the

Wheat field, road to Onil

Church domes, Jijona

Turks, led to the fear of invasion and a chain of watchtowers and fortresses all along the coast, as seen at Santa Pola and Campello.

A further serious blow was the expulsion of the *moriscos,* the Muslims who had stayed after the Reconquest and provided an invaluable skilled workforce in the towns and on the land. At first they were largely free to follow their old customs and language, but from the early 16th century they became a scapegoat for economic problems. Growing enmity and suspicion found ritual voice in forced conversions and, finally, culminated in expulsion in 1609 by Philip III, who wanted to break the power of the Valencian nobles. Initially, the Murcian *moriscos* were exempted because of their importance to the economy, but a few years later they, too, were expelled. A long economic and cultural recession resulted and the region did not recover fully till the 18th century.

With the drawn-out War of Succession of 1702–14 and the accession to the throne of Philip V – the first of the Bourbon monarchs – the political map was redrawn. Many cities and towns in Valencia, which had backed Charles, Archduke of Austria, lost their rights – Játiva was even burned to the ground. In contrast, areas that had solidly supported the Bourbon cause, such as Murcia and Alicante, benefited from royal favour. In the century that followed, the economic potential of natural resources began to be realised for the first time since the Reconquest. Reservoirs, windmills and aqueducts were built to irrigate arid areas; forest was cleared to plant vines, olives and cereals; the lower Segura valley was drained to become fertile *huerta* and broken into aristocratic or monastic estates. Workshops producing silk and other textiles flourished in both Murcia and Alicante, and, in the middle of the century, industrial techniques appeared in Alcoy. Public works programmes and Genoese traders helped the ports to develop; Cartagena became a major defensive arsenal; and Alicante soon boasted the third-largest volume of trade in Spain.

The region's new wealth and confidence was expressed in a massive building boom that incorporated a late flowering of baroque

Alicante costume

architecture. Palaces and señorial houses acquired ornate façades; churches were topped by blue-tiled cupolas like teapot lids; Murcia, Lorca and Orihuela were remodelled, with a new synthesis of religious and secular space. The decorative thrust – which also found expression in the forum of fiestas and costume – reflected a dynamic society with a growing influence from Castile rather than Valencia.

Throughout the 19th century, this economic development and the parallel creation of a new middle class continued, checked temporarily by the War of Independence against the French and an earthquake in the Segura valley, quickened by the confiscation and redistribution of monastery estates and barely interrupted by the wars between the liberals and conservatives. The new provincial boundaries of the 1830s marked the beginning of Orihuela's decline and Alicante's rise as a local capital. Improved transport brought new markets for agricultural produce and the first tourists, while industrialisation – largely in Alcoy and Cartagena – trailed political radicalism and mining wealth in its wake. During the first Republic of 1873, anarchist workers at Alcoy seized the town, killed the mayor and the Guardia Civil, while at Cartagena, cantonalists seeking regional secession introduced divorce and abolished the death penalty before being bombarded into submission. Mining wealth left its mark in some fine Modernist architecture (at Cartagena, Jumilla, Alcoy, La Unión and Novelda, where there is a small museum).

For all this, rural 19th-century life kept a highly localised quality defined by physical horizons. The vineyard regions around Monóvar, Denia, Yecla and Jumilla, which boomed briefly when phylloxera destroyed French vines; the poor fishing and smuggling villages, such as Benidorm or Torrevieja; the green *huerta* of the Segura valley, its adobe *barracas* periodically swept away by flooding; the harsh northern valleys, where life still centred on the old *morisco* hamlets; the southern Campo de Cartagena, where windmills drew up water and ground wheat – all these geographical pockets lived as worlds apart from one another.

As they became sucked into the international marketplace, there was a major economic crisis on the land. At the turn of the century, vineyards and olive groves were torn up to make way for citrus fruit and almonds. Drought and flooding periodically tipped the balance over into major disaster. The poverty never became as desperate as that of the south – the wealth of the *huertas* and the shared inheritance system meant there were always more self-sufficient property owners than labourers – but the flow of emigration to local cities, North Africa and Catalunya was steady and, in bad years like the early 1930s, it rose to a flood.

The Civil War

When civil war broke out in 1936, Murcia and the Levante (eastern Spain) declared for Republicanism and sent brigades to the military fronts even though they remained rearguard areas. At home, many churches were looted and major cities bombarded. The collectivisation of land followed apace. After the fall of Madrid and the Republican government in Valencia the region finally fell to the Nationalists in 1939.

Art Nouveau church at La Mola near Novelda

The postwar decade under Franco's military dictatorship saw painfully slow reconstruction by an exhausted country. Not until the 1950s did the economy strengthen and the gap close between town and country, inland and coastal areas. Driving through here in the late 1940s, Rose Macaulay wrote, 'This is a haunted shore: ghosts around each bay, each little town, each castled rock, whispering in the lap of waves and in the low rumour of the sea wind in the palms.' Ten years later, the tourist invasion was underway and the shoreline of Alicante and Murcia had become known as the Costa Blanca.

The first real boom, with accompanying rampant property speculation, happened in the 1960s: skyscrapers replaced the old inns and the number of visitors to Alicante province shot up to over 3 million a year. Smaller but significant booms followed in the 1970s and 1980s, spreading down the coast to the Mar Menor and inland to the valleys and sierras. Apart from the transformation of the landscape and local economy, tourism also became a major cultural phenomenon in the 1960s, bringing social liberalisation and creating a new bourgeoisie long before Franco's death and the arrival of democracy in 1978.

Despite the pressure of tourism, industry and agriculture have continued to grow. Industry – partly based on traditional crafts and partly imported with oil refineries and the like – gives work to more than a quarter of the population. And although agriculture is shrinking away from resorts, it has thrived elsewhere – especially the Murcian *huerta,* called the market garden of Europe; Alicante is the fourth wealthiest province in Spain.

With the ghost of postwar poverty fading away, concern for the environment has emerged as a major issue among Spaniards. In the Costa Blanca area, local indicators, such as falling fishing catches, high levels of pollution in Cartagena, soil erosion and dropping water tables, have highlighted the importance of ecological balance in an area that has always struggled against natural disaster. The limited response so far – protection of large areas of countryside, stricter controls on heavy industry and official backing for 'green' tourism – is likely to be followed by more extensive changes. The region's water supply is forecast to dry up within 10 years unless massive hydraulics projects tap the supplies of other regions.

A second theme of contemporary life has been the revival of every aspect of regional culture – language, fiestas, cooking, dance and music – and a revaluation of the rapidly disappearing 'old' Spain alongside new social patterns for the future. With its decentralised economy, high proportion of foreign residents and multilingual society, the Costa Blanca is already the integrated Europe of which many politicians dream.

Farmer off to work near Moratalla

Historical Highlights

c50,000BC First evidence of cave dwellings (Cueva del Cochino, Villena; Cueva de las Calaveres, Benidoleig).

8th century Phoenician traders introduce the pottery wheel, the fig and the olive.

223 Quart Hades founded on site of Cartagena.

218–09 Roman army, under Publio Cornelio Scipio, conquers Spanish Mediterranean coast, from Emporias to the Carthaginian capital, Quart Hades, which they rename Cartago Nova.

AD555 Byzantine troops conquer Cartago, but lose all their territory to Visigoths by 624.

711–14 Muslims invade and conquer Iberian peninsula, except for areas in the northwest.

756 Caliphate of Córdoba founded.

1010–95 *Taifa* kingdoms in power (in this area, Denia and Murcia).

1095 Almoravides, Berbers from the Atlas mountains, invade.

1160 Another Berber tribe, the Almohades, invade.

13th C The Reconquest moves southwards in a two-pronged drive by Castile and Aragon.

1243–4 Kingdom of Murcia ceded by Ben-Hud dynasty to Castile.

1238–48 James I of Aragon conquers northern Alicante.

1263 Muslim rebellion in Murcia put down by James I of Aragon.

1276 Muslim revolt in Alicante finally quashed.

1304 Treaty of Torrellas confirms Alicante's annexation of Castilian territory south to Mar Menor.

1361 Pedro the Cruel takes Alicante for Castile after repeated attempts (his brother Henry II of Trastamara returns it after Pedro's death).

1474 Ferdinand and Isabella marry to unite Castile and Aragon, but the states keep separate legal systems.

1492 Fall of Muslim Granada. The expulsion of the Spanish Jews.

1519 Revolt against nobility and persecution of *moriscos* (converted Muslims) in kingdom of Valencia.

1609 Expulsion of *moriscos.*

1702–14 Spanish War of Succession between Philip of Anjou (V) and Charles, Duke of Hapsburg.

1783 Death of Francisco Salzillo, Baroque sculptor.

1808–12 War of Independence (Peninsula War) against the French.

1812 A Spanish constitution written.

1829 Earthquake destroys towns of lower Segura valley.

1833–6 Present provincial boundaries fixed: Villena, Denia and Orihuela included in Alicante province.

1858 Alicante to Madrid railway line opens.

1862 Railway line from Madrid to Murcia city opens.

1873 First Republic: *cantanolismo* (secession) in Cartagena.

1888 In Cartagena, Isaac Peral builds what is claimed to be the world's first working submarine.

1936–9 Civil War: Alicante and Murcia remain Republican.

1939 Surrender to the Nationalists after fall of Madrid.

1960–71 Number of visitors annually to Alicante province rises from 950,000 to over 3,750,000.

1982 Statutes of Autonomy of Valencia and Murcia regions.

Mid 1980s Spain has the fastest growing economy in western Europe.

Early 1990s Recession kicks in.

1995 Regional government elections: Partido Popular (conservative) wins power in Valencia and Murcia.

Costa Blanca North
16 km / 10 miles
Paterna
Burjassot
R. Turia
Valencia
Gulf of Valencia
Palma de Mallorca
Torrent
Pinedo
Catarroja
Silla
Picassent
La Albufera
Elvissa (Ibiza)
El Palmar
Benifaió
Laguna de la Plana
El Perelló
Alginet
Canal Júcar-Turia
Las Palmeras
Carlet
Sueca
Balsa de S. Lorenzo
Algemesí
Cullera
Alzira
Corbera
Mediterranean Sea
Favara
Alberique
Carcaixent
R. Júcar
Tabernes
Vilanova
Casa de Alcade
Alcàntera de Xúquer
Rafelguaraf
Simat de Valldigna
R. Barxeta
Barxeta
SIERRA DE GANDIA
El Grao de Gandia
Xàtiva (Játiva)
Gandía
Canals
Llutxent
Palma de Gandia
Guadasequies
Oliva
Castelló de Rugat
Morqui
R. Serpis
Posada San Jaime
Montaberner
Villalonga
R. Micena
Elvissa (Ibiza)
Bovetes
Denia
Lorcha
Albaida
Pego
Ondara
Les Rotas
Embalse de Beniarrés
Ontinyent
Cueva de las Calaveras
Alcalá de la Iovada
Xàbia (Jávea)
Mare de Deu d' Agres
Planes
PLAYA DE MAR AZOL
SIERRA DE ALFARO
Gata de Gorgos
Agres
Benimarfull
Xaló (Jalón)
ISLA DE PORTIXOL
Bocairent
Cocentaina
Parcent
Lliber
Benitachell
Coll de Rates
Teulada
Cabo de la Nao
SIERRA DE MARIOLA
Benissa
Embalse de Guadalest (reservoir)
PLAYA DE LA GRANADELLA
Castillo de Guadalest
Tárberna
Alcoi (Alcoy)
Benasau
Beniarda
Punta de Moraira
Confrides
Guadalest
Fonts de Algar
Penàguila
Alcolecha
Benimantell
Calpe
Callosa d' Ensarria
Altea la Vieja (vella)
Peñón d' Ifach
Benifallim
SIERRA DE AITANA
Polop
Ibi
R. Amadorio
Sella
Altea
SIERRA DE LA PENYA ROSSA
Torremanzanas
SIERRA DE ORCHETA
Relleu
Punta Bombarda
Cueva de Canalobre
Embalse de Relleu
Benidorm
Jijona
Embalse de Amadorio
Punta de la Escaleta
Tibi
Villajoyosa (La Vila Joiosa)
Embalse de Tibi
Busot
R. Monnegre
Day 1
Day 2
Itinerary 1 (from Alicante)
Itinerary 2
Itinerary 3
Itinerary 5
Itinerary 4: Benidorm

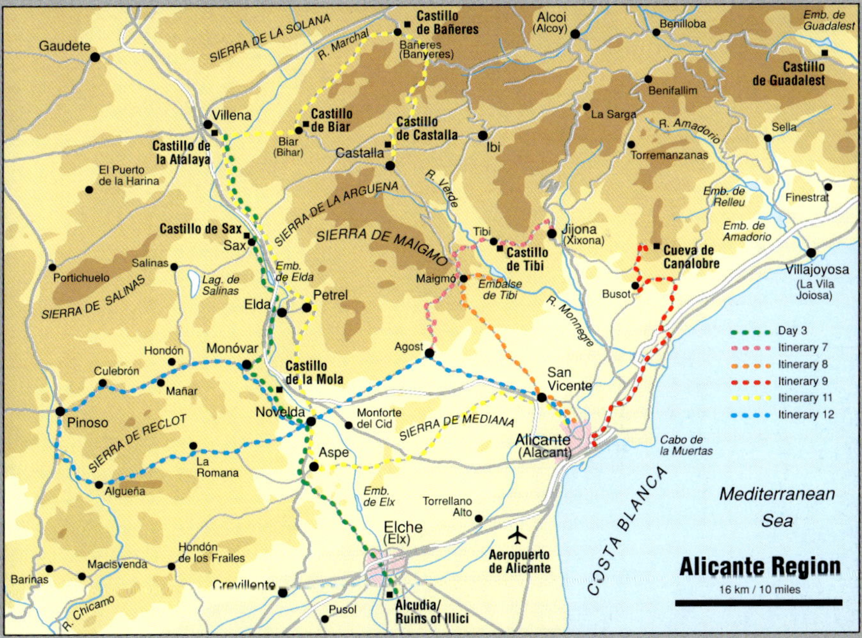
Alicante Region
16 km / 10 miles
Day 3
Itinerary 7
Itinerary 8
Itinerary 9
Itinerary 11
Itinerary 12
Mediterranean Sea
COSTA BLANCA
Gaudete
SIERRA DE LA SOLANA
R. Marchal
Castillo de Bañeres
Bañeres (Banyeres)
Alcoi (Alcoy)
Benilloba
Emb. de Guadalest
Castillo de Guadalest
Benifallim
Villena
Castillo de Biar
Biar (Bihar)
Castillo de Castalla
Castalla
Ibi
La Sarga
R. Amadorio
Sella
Torremanzanas
Castillo de la Atalaya
El Puerto de la Harina
SIERRA DE LA ARGUENA
R. Verde
Emb. de Relleu
Finestrat
Emb. de Amadorio
Castillo de Sax
Sax
SIERRA DE MAIGMO
Tibi
Castillo de Tibi
Jijona (Xixona)
Cueva de Canalobre
Villajoyosa (La Vila Joiosa)
Portichuelo
Salinas
Lag. de Salinas
Emb. de Elda
Petrel
Maigmo
Embalse de Tibi
Busot
SIERRA DE SALINAS
Elda
R. Monnegre
Hondón
Monóvar
Castillo de la Mola
Agost
Culebrón
Mañar
San Vicente
Pinoso
Novelda
Monforte del Cid
SIERRA DE RECLOT
SIERRA DE MEDIANA
Alicante (Alacant)
Cabo de la Muertas
La Romana
Aspe
Algueña
Emb. de Elx
Torrellano Alto
Elche (Elx)
Aeropuerto de Alicante
Hondón de los Frailes
Macisvenda
Barinas
Crevillente
R. Chicamo
Pusol
Alcudia/ Ruins of Illici

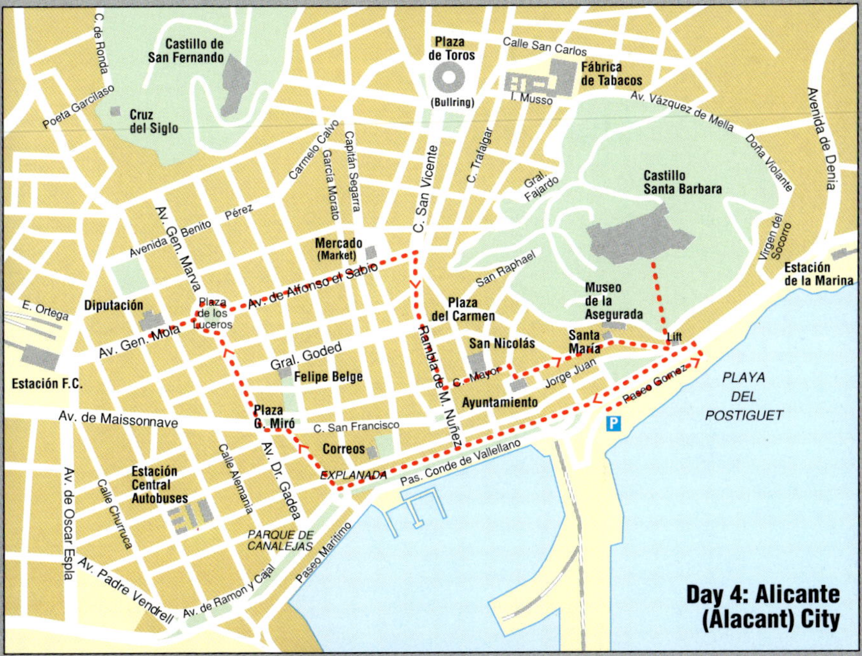
Day 4: Alicante (Alacant) City
C. de Ronda
Castillo de San Fernando
Plaza de Toros
(Bullring)
Calle San Carlos
Fábrica de Tabacos
I. Musso
Av. Vázquez de Mella
Avenida de Denia
Poeta Garcilaso
Cruz del Siglo
Carmelo Calvo
García Morato
Capitán Segarra
C. San Vicente
C. Trafalgar
Gral. Fajardo
Doña Violante
Castillo Santa Barbara
Avenida Benito Pérez
Av. Gen. Marva
Mercado (Market)
San Raphael
Virgen del Socorro
Estación de la Marina
Av. de Alfonso el Sabio
E. Ortega
Diputación
Plaza de los Luceros
Plaza del Carmen
Museo de la Asegurada
Av. Gen. Mola
Rambla de M. Nuñez
San Nicolás
Santa María
Lift
Gral. Goded
Estación F.C.
Felipe Belge
C. Mayor
Jorge Juan
Paseo Gomez
PLAYA DEL POSTIGUET
Ayuntamiento
Plaza G. Miró
Av. de Maissonnave
C. San Francisco
P
Correos
Calle Alemania
Av. Dr. Gadea
EXPLANADA
Pas. Conde de Vallellano
Av. de Oscar Espla
Estación Central Autobuses
Calle Churruca
PARQUE DE CANALEJAS
Paseo Marítimo
Av. Padre Vendrell
Av. de Ramon y Cajal

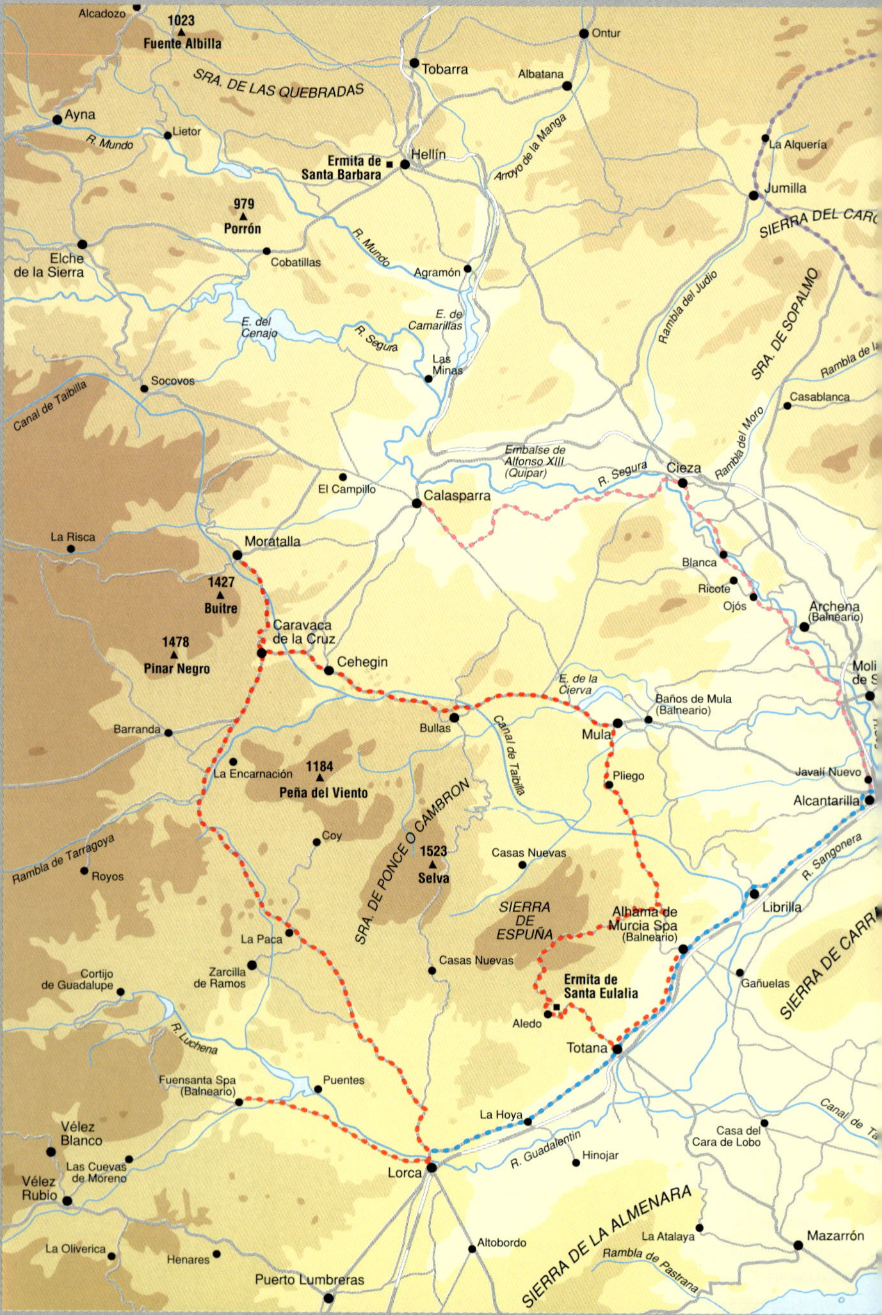

Alcadozo
1023
Fuente Albilla
Ontur
Tobarra
Albatana
SRA. DE LAS QUEBRADAS
Ayna
R. Mundo
Lietor
Arroyo de la Manga
La Alquería
Ermita de Santa Barbara
Hellín
Jumilla
979
Porrón
SIERRA DEL CAR
Elche de la Sierra
Cobatillas
R. Mundo
Agramón
E. de Camarillas
E. del Cenajo
R. Segura
Rambla del Judío
SRA. DE SOPALMO
Las Minas
Socovos
Canal de Taibilla
Rambla de la
Casablanca
Rambla del Moro
Embalse de Alfonso XIII (Quipar)
R. Segura
Cieza
El Campillo
Calasparra
La Risca
Moratalla
Blanca
1427
Buitre
Ricote
Ojós
Archena (Balneario)
1478
Pinar Negro
Caravaca de la Cruz
Cehegin
E. de la Cierva
Baños de Mula (Balneario)
Bullas
Canal de Taibilla
Mula
Barranda
La Encarnación
1184
Peña del Viento
Pliego
Javalí Nuevo
Alcantarilla
SRA. DE PONCE O CAMBRON
Coy
1523
Selva
Casas Nuevas
Rambla de Tarragoya
Royos
R. Sangonera
Librilla
SIERRA DE ESPUÑA
Alhama de Murcia Spa (Balneario)
La Paca
Casas Nuevas
SIERRA DE CARR
Cortijo de Guadalupe
Zarcilla de Ramos
Ermita de Santa Eulalia
Gañuelas
Aledo
Totana
R. Luchena
Fuensanta Spa (Balneario)
Puentes
La Hoya
Canal de Ta
Vélez Blanco
Las Cuevas de Moreno
R. Guadalentín
Hinojar
Casa del Cara de Lobo
Lorca
Vélez Rubio
SIERRA DE LA ALMENARA
La Atalaya
Mazarrón
La Oliverica
Henares
Altobordo
Rambla de Pastrana
Puerto Lumbreras

Castalla
Relleu
E. de Relleu
E. de Amadorio
SRA. DE LA SERRETA
Sax
SRA. DE MAIGMO
Jijona (Xixona)
Cueva de Canalobre
Villajoyosa (La Vila Joiosa)
Portichuelo
Embalse de Tibi
R. Monnegre
Elda
Petrel
Agost
Monóvar
San Vicente
Pinoso
Novelda
Castillo
Las Cuevas
Aspe
Alicante (Alacant)
Cabo de las Huertas
835
Crevillente
Elche (Elx)
Barinas
Crevillente
R. Chicamo
Abanilla
Santa Pola
Fortuna
ISLA DE TABARCA
Saladar del Ajanque
Callosa
Orihuela (Oriola)
R. Segura
Guardamar del Segura
Bigastro
Desamparados
Jacarilla
Beniel
Salinas de La Mata
E. de la Pedrena
Alqueirías
Salinas de Torrevieja
Murcia
COSTA BLANCA
Mediterranean Sea
San Miguel de Salinas
Torrevieja
Santuardio de Fuensanta
Dehesa de Campoamor
Sucina
os Baños
San Pedro del Pinatar
Los Martinez
San Javier
Punta del Pudrider
Torre-Pacheco
Los Alcázares
Balsa-Pintada
Manga del Mar Menor
Mar Menor
Alamo
PL. DE LOS METOS
La Palma
Cabo de Palos
Cuesta Blanca
Algar
MPO DE CARTAGENA
Cartagena
La Unión
Los Velones
Portman
Calblanque
Cabo Negrete
Azohía
Day 5
Day 6
Day 7
Itinerary 10
Itinerary 13
Itinerary 14
Itinerary 15: Murcia
Itinerary 16: Cartagena
Costa Blanca South and Murcia
16 km / 10 miles

Guide to the Guide

Insight Pocket Guide: Costa Blanca is based on a series of itineraries designed to show you the best of the coast and its hinterland.

It begins with seven itineraries, each a day's duration, covering the principal towns of the region, all of which can be reached from the resorts along the coast from Denia to Torrevieja.

The 'Pick and Mix' section offers a further 16 itineraries that explore the region in greater detail, allowing you to create your own travel programme, depending upon your particular interests and energy.

You will not have time to follow all the suggestions in one short trip – but it is hoped you will enjoy this area of great beauty and extraordinary contrasts so much that you will return again soon, to continue exploring where you left off.

A Note on Language

Since 1982 Alicante province has been bilingual along with the rest of the autonomous region of Valencia. *Valenciano* – now on an equal legal footing with *castellano* (or Spanish) after years of suppression under Franco – is a written and spoken language closely related to Catalan. *Valenciano* has its own literature and is now the language of local government, as well as regional television and radio. Murcia uses only *castellano*, though sometimes with the dying local dialect of *panocho*.

On an everyday spoken basis, however, the reality is more complex than this. The northern third of Alicante province remains solidly *valenciano* speaking and another wedge in the south – around Elche and the Segura valley – is rapidly becoming so now that young people are learning *valenciano* at school. However, *castellano* continues to dominate in Alicante city, the Vinalopo valley, Orihuela and other border areas with Murcia and, of course, in many of the coastal resorts. Road and street signs, maps, local newspapers and other printed information reflect this regional shading and are not yet consistently bilingual.

As a result, *Insight Pocket Guide: Costa Blanca* is not entirely consistent either. City and town listings give both *castellano* and *valenciano* placenames where they differ (for example, Elche and Elx) and names of museums and restaurants are given as they were found. In general references within the text, both are used as appropriate to the context, although *castellano* tends to occur more frequently than *valenciano*.

DAY 1

Sunrise to Sunset on the Northern Coast: Calpe to the Col de Rates

Allow 4 hours for the Peñón d'Ifach (a rocky coastal outcrop), the small town of Benissa and a beach. An afternoon drive (2½ hours with stops) loops back into wine country and up to a sierra viewpoint before dinner in a country restaurant. *See map on page 24.*

The coastline of the northern Alicante province, **La Marina**, is heavily developed as up-market family resorts, with a ribbon of villas running between them. But dotted around, between and behind the development are unspoiled pockets with areas of lovely countryside and, in the towns and villages, reminders of a long history of piracy and invasion. Start at **Calpe** (Calp), dubbed 'Muy Heroica Villa' by Charles V for its stoic defence against Berber pirates. Just outside the town, which is overrun by tourism, is the **Peñón d'Ifach**, a huge limestone fang rearing out of the sea. Charted in ancient times by Hercules and later used as a watchtower, it is now a symbol for the Costa Blanca, overlooking crowded beaches on either side but still keeping its splendid isolation.

The easiest parking place is in the fishing port below. From there it is a long climb up – the Peñón is 330m (1,083ft) high – through a tunnel in the bottom of the rock face (allow 30–40mins). It is worth the effort though, since the views over the coastline are superb, especially at sunrise. The slopes and rocky bays below are worth clambering over too; they are now a *parque natural* protecting over 300 plant species – including a unique orchid and carnation

Benissa

– which grow in the sheltered micro-climate. In summer, make sure you are back down at the bottom before the heat of the day (the study centre has a convenient bar).

From the Peñón, cut back inland to **Benissa**, a town built several miles inland for safety from pirate attacks, with *rejas*, iron grills, over the windows. Everything of interest here is in one, long narrow strip running from the top to the bottom of the town. At the very top, in Calle Escoto, the Franciscan **Convento de los Capuchinos**, founded in 1611, is built of soft golden stone (ring on the doorbell to visit). Lower down, in the centre of town, the **Calle de la Purísima** is lined with lovely old medieval houses, often with old porches and gable designs of Moorish origin, and the 15th-century agricultural exchange houses a **Museu de Etnografía** (July and August 10am–1pm and 5–7pm; or by arrangement). Opposite you can pick up a late breakfast or mid-morning snack at a knock-out bakery, **Bolufer**.

Make your way back to the coast via Teulada and Benitachell, where smaller roads and tracks run down past holiday housing to the beaches around the **Cabo de la Nao (Cap de la Nau)**. The most spectacular of these is the Cala de los Tiestos, an enclosed golden strip sheltered by tall cliffs reached through the Cumbrel del Sol estate. Swimming here is a double-edged pleasure since the beach was made accessible by developers blasting their way down through the headland in 1982; the brash estate they are still building has spread into a monstrous blot on the landscape and threatens the local marine life. Less abrasive are **Platja de la Granadell**, further round, or the **Playa de Mar Azul**, looking over the tiny Isla de Portitxol. It has good snorkelling, a diving pontoon and a couple of breezy beach bars.

Outside beach weather, it is easy to while away an hour or two in **Xàbia (Jávea)**. It has a fine fortified Gothic church, its tawny stones softened and pockmarked by salt winds. The nearby **museum** (C. Primicias 1; Tuesday to Sunday 10am–1pm; July to September, also 6–9pm) is intelligently laid out and neatly slices through the history of the coast from Palaeolithic caves and Iberian villages to Roman wealth and medieval poverty. It also has a good collection of Moorish ceramics and craft equipment, such as *alpargata* tools and a raisin press. From here, it is a short drive up past the deserted terraces of the small **Serra del Montgó** and the Torre de Cero, a 16th-century watchtower, to the fish restaurants of **Denia**. (As you come down into the bay take a sharp right, marked for Les Rotes, and then look for signs.) They are famed for their *arros abanda*, rice cooked in a rock and shellfish stock flavoured with saffron and *sofrito*. It may look plain next to most tourist *paellas*, but it knocks them into a cocked hat. **El Pegolí**, one of several such restaurants, is particularly memorable (*see page 91*). From here you can drive down to to **Les Roques**, the old fishing quarter, where the day's catch is auctioned at 5pm.

In the late afternoon loop back into the olive and citrus groves, stopping off quickly for a glimpse of **Ondara's** wonderful small bullring. Access is through the Bar Plaza de Toros: tickets for the fights (July and August) go quickly and need to be bought well in advance. A short drive on, you can stop at **Gata de Gorgos'** cane and wickerwork shops (much of the stock is now imported). At Gata turn off to **Llibér**, driving through rolling hills into the well-tamed wine country of the **Gorgos valley**. As you approach **Xaló (Jalón)**, the soil turns from red to yellow and vineyards begin to cover the valley floor. They were once famed for their sweet malmsey made from muscatel grapes and their raisins. Today the vineyards are still dotted by the characteristic *riu-raus*, arched porches used for drying the grapes, but they are hardly used. Xaló itself is a tranquil town dominated by a vast 19th-century church, with a good wine cooperative where you can taste and buy the claret-like red and excellent sweet muscatel wines. From here, drive on up to the **Col de Rates** – signposted for Tárberna and Callosa – a bare lookout point (780m/2,559ft) with great views.

Immediately below is **Parcent**, a dozy village where life rotates around the agricultural cooperative and its splendid *fin-de-siglo* bar. Stop off here for a local wine or *mosto* – unfermented grape juice – before backtracking to Llibér to finish the long day with supper at the **Terrases de la Torre**, a relaxed country restaurant serving excellent local dishes (*see page 92*).

Col de Rates

DAY 2

The Northern Hill Towns and Sierra de Aitana

A 1½ hour drive from the lush coast behind Benidorm takes you past a waterfall and hill villages to two inland towns with historic centres: Cocentaina and Alcoi. The drive back (1½ hours) crosses high sierras with spectacular views. *See map on page 24.*

In the northern sierras, all roads seem to lead to **Alcoi (Alcoy)**. Sited in a sheltered river plain where a number of rivers converge behind the coastal hills, it is both the oldest and largest of the northern hill towns, the original Iberian hill top settlement looking down on modern textile and paper factories which grew out of Moorish workshops. This itinerary takes you there via the valley road and **Concentaina**, a close historic neighbour, and back over the **Sierra de Aitana**. To see everything along the way, you need to make an early start and move on snappily from one sight to the other. Or, for a more leisurely day, make a choice of destinations before you start.

Start at the **Fonts de Algar**, where the river of the same name rises just outside **Callosa de Ensarriá** (take the road to Tárberna and follow the signs; there is a large car park). Buried in a jungly-green valley filled with citrus and medlar groves, the water alternates between cascades and pools, running between river banks covered with pink oleander and bougainvillaea in summer. Starting at the lowest and most spectacular waterfall and natural bathing pool, you can climb up alongside the river for 20mins or so until it becomes a mountain stream and then, where the path runs out, wade on up to the top.

Fonts de Algar

Suitably cooled down, drive on to Alcoi past Guadalest and Confrides. The lush frondiness drops away together with the sub-tropical micro-climate and the road winds between harsh sierras until you reach the chalky plateau of Alcoi. Just after Benilloba, take the right

turn to **Cocentaina** (20 mins). One of the least written up but most interesting historic towns of the province, it has clearly delineated medieval Christian and Jewish quarters on either side of the **Palau del Comtat**, a golden-walled 15th to 16th-century fortified palace.

Slowly being restored from a badly decayed state, the palace is now open to the public (Monday to Saturday 11am–7pm and Monday to Friday 5–10pm; informal guided tour, 30mins, no charge). Long-term plans include the return of furnishings from the Casa de Pilate in Seville and museum space for the wealth of Iberian, Roman and Moorish finds made in the locality. In the meantime, the chapel with the **Mare de Déu**, a painting of the Virgin Mary which miraculously burst into tears, and some rooms with fine wooden ceilings and tiled floors, are fragments of the former – and perhaps future – magnificence of the palace.

The **Sala Dorada**, the Palau del Comtat's most richly decorated room, situated on its western corner, is dedicated to the wartime victories of the Aragonese crown. The neighbouring **Convento de Clarisas** (8am–12pm and 5–7pm) is also worth a quick peep inside for its collection of fine paintings, which include a 15th-century Byzantine *retablo*.

After such a long and energetic morning, the nearby **Venta del Pilar** is an excellent place in which to relax over a leisurely lunch. Dishes are substantial and in the after-lunch gap, when everything other than bars and restaurants is closed, you can sit over an *eaux-de-vie* (*see page 91*). A hot-weather alternative is a picnic at **Font Roja**, a 20-minutes' drive on the other side of Alcoi. The 19th-century chapel is superbly sited next to an icy water source and a former health spa converted into a government *parador*. From here, paths lead up into a large area of parkland protecting indigenous Mediterranean woods.

Late afternoon, when the streets are coming back to life, is the perfect time to arrive in **Alcoi**. As you approach from Cocentaina over the suspension bridge, the town's geography is at its most dramatic, with houses appearing to topple down into a gorge cut by the meeting of rivers. The town centre is quite distinct from others in the province, with a secular 19th-century air reflecting its early industrialisation: hence the old-fashioned banks and shops (for example in **Calle Juan Cantó**), the frilly Modernist balconies and workers' cultural centres, and the five bridges. All of these date from the end of the last century and were built with the profits from the cotton industry.

The open spaces are thoroughly 19th-century too. La Bandeja, as the main Plaça d'Espanya is nicknamed, is heavy and grandiose; but the smaller neighbouring **Plaça de Dins**, where doves flutter around over the site of the convent torn down in the 1820s, and the nearby **Glorieta**, a park with peacocks and a tall dovecote, are charming and amusing places to observe well-dressed provincial Spanish life.

Plaça de Dins, Alcoi

Below the main square is the graceful, if down-at-heel, old core of the town. The 17th-century town hall houses the local archaeological museum, whose exhibits include a small lead tablet with writing in an undeciphered Iberian alphabet and the Iberian Dama de Jerreta; **Museu Arqueologic Municipal** (Monday to Friday 10am–2pm, Saturday, Sunday and holidays 10.30am–1.30pm).

Nearby is the **Museu de Festes**, the private museum of the town's rumbustious Moors and Christians fiesta (C. San Miguel 60, Tuesday to Friday 11.30am–1.30pm and 5.30–7.30pm, weekends 11.30am–1.30pm; small charge for entry). To an outsider, the pomp of the fiesta costumes and paraphernalia that goes with them is extraordinary; to the people of Alcoi, it is a matter of both great pride and of economic interest, since many of the factories making these and costumes for other traditional fiestas around the country are based here.

To return to the coast and presumably to your base, take the mountain road over the **Sierra de Aitana** via the villages of Benilloba, **Penaguila** – worth a look – and **Rellen**, a lovely unspoilt village from which you can walk to an Arab castle (ask locally). There are paths up into the mountains, semi-alpine flora and some fine views here, plus a couple of bars where you can have a drink while watching the sun set and even stay on for a homely supper. Alternatively, you could wait until you reach the coast at **Villajoyosa (La Vila Joiosa)**, where you can choose from a clutch of good fish restaurants.

This itinerary would link up well with the short evening trip in the Guadalest valley (*see Pick & Mix 5, page 60*), or the two-day itinerary in the Gallinera and Agres valleys (*see Pick & Mix 3, page 57*).

DAY 3

Villena and Elche: Buried History

A morning visit to the Iberian gold collection at Villena, a 30-minute drive from Alicante (there are also frequent trains); in the afternoon a 45-minute drive to the Iberian–Roman site outside Elche, plus Europe's largest palm forest in the town centre. *See map on page 25.*

At a first glance, **Villena** and **Elche** – or **Elx** in *valenciano* – have little in common: Villena is a bustling small town in the Vinalopó valley, known for the silhouette of its medieval castle and for the strength of its wine; Elche is a dusty city, associated with its date palm forest, mystery play and mushrooming shoe factories. Under the surface though – quite literally – the two share buried treasures, brought to light in the last century. It was in 1897 that farm workers stumbled upon the Dama de Elche, the sculpture which has since become a symbol of the sophistication of Iberian culture. Unfortunately for Elche, the Dama, serenely enigmatic, made her way via dealers to Paris and then back to Madrid, where she maintains pride of place in the Museo Arquelógico (and it has been made clear that she will not be returned to her place of origin). Since then, however, many more riches have been turned up on the same Iberian and Roman site, where the river city of Illici stood. These Elche has kept.

Villena takes us even further back – another 50,000 or so years. Start the day here in the lovely 17th-century *ayuntamiento*, where the **Museo Arqueológico** (Pl. Santiago 1, Tuesday to Friday 10am–2pm and 5–8pm; tel: 96 580 1150, ext 66; Weekends 11am–1pm, telephone first) is squeezed into one room. It is the life's work of one man, José María Soler, now in his eighties. The star attraction is an extraordinary Iberian treasure-trove of 30 pieces of solid fluvial gold – bowls and small pots moulded and beaten to look like sea urchins, stunningly beautiful necklaces, bracelets weighing up to half a kilo (2 lbs) each and giant earstuds. These Soler found one weekend in the mid-1960s when he was still a civil servant working for the Post Office.

José María Soler and the Villena gold

Cathedral, Elche

Soler is quick to point out the importance of the rest of the collection, which often gets overlooked. It comes from a large number of nearby sites, one of them the Bronze Age capital of Cabeza Redonda – where the treasure was found – and another, called the Casa de Lara, unique in that it straddles 8,000 years of history and technological development. Other gems, include a second (smaller) gold 'treasure', a unique clay crucible and a drinking bottle with a double mouth, perhaps for *anís* and water.

While in Villena, do not miss the 15th- and 16th-century church of **Santiago**, one of the finest examples of Levantine Gothic in Alicante province: its fluted cable columns, topped by lovely floral capitals, soar on up into high, shadowy vaulting, and next to the altar is a wonderful, richly carved font, also 16th-century, by sculptor Jacopo Florentino, one of Michelangelo's assistants, who moved to Spain and settled in Villena. (The font spent many years in a back-room because the priest objected to the bared breasts displayed around the outside.) Providing a service isn't in progress, enter the church through the chapel on the far side from the *plaza*. You can also climb up, past the rich baroque facade of the **Iglesia de Santa María**, to the severe castle (*see page 69*).

The route on to Elche passes close to **Monóvar** (*see page 70*), where there are a number of good country restaurants serving the local *gazpachos* and rice with snails, washed down by the strong local wines.

It is then only half-an-hour's drive to the **Museo Monográfico de Alcudia**, on the site of **Illici**, one of Spain's most important Iberian sites (entry times vary; ask at the tourist information office in Elche before visiting. Small admission charge; badly signposted in town – follow signs to Dolores and watch for the turn-off at 2.2km). Again, the museum is a labour of love, this time by the Ramos family who own the farm and have produced three generations of archaeologists. Astonishingly, given the value of the site, only one-tenth of it has yet been excavated, although the family organises digs each summer. The 3,000 pieces on show and the highlights of the site itself deserve at least an hour.

Back in the dusty city centre, housed in the east wing of the **Alcázar de la Senoría/Palacio de Altamira** (Tuesday to Friday 10am–1pm and 4–7pm; weekends and holidays 10am–1pm) is the town's own **Museo Arqueológico**, where prize pieces from Alcudia are on show: for example, two prowling sphinxes and a headless Roman Venus. The Palacio's walls and towers are also open. From here it is a short walk through to the other monuments in the historic centre: the Moorish **Calaforra**, or watchtower, with its extraordinary *mudéjar* hallway; just beyond, the 16th-century facade of the **Convento de la Mercè**, inside which are Moorish baths (these cannot be visited); the *ayuntamiento*, with its 14th-century jacquemard clock striking on the quarter; and finally, dominating everything else, the baroque **Basílica**, its weighty dimensions those of a cathedral (Tuesday–Sunday 7am–1.30pm and 5.30–9pm). Here, the **Misterio de Elche**, the only mystery play still performed in a Catholic church, takes place every August.

The glorious small monastery church of **San José**, a 15-minute walk away on the far side of the river, is well worth the effort for its refreshingly humble Franciscan version of baroque, with original frescoes, *azulejos* and woodcarving. You can stroll there and back over La Pasarela and through the former Moorish quarter, or Raval, marked out by its tightly packed streets, finishing up at La Glorieta for a refreshing drink before finally going on to the **Hort del Cura**, the botanical garden within the palm forest (Tuesday–Sunday 9am–8pm; admission charge).

The Hort, which was laid out by a priest in the last century, is most famous for the Imperial Palm, a hermaphrodite palm tree that changed sex after about 70 years of life and sprouted seven new trunks, one of which produces dates. But for many it is the artfulness of the planting between the palms, the contrasts between cactuses and lilies, which makes the garden so seductive.

Tailoring supper to the size of your pocket, you can choose between various restaurants in the centre or on the edge of town (*for details see page 92*), where you can try the great local speciality of *arroz con costra*, rice with pork and sausages buried under a golden egg crust.

Imperial Palm Tree, Elche

DAY 4

Alicante City

A full day exploring Alicante on foot: the castle, museum and old town in the morning; a beach in the afternoon; the small museum of 20th-century art in the early evening. *See map of Alicante on page 25.*

Alicante (Alacant) is by no means only a tourist capital. Where the beaches end, a Mediterranean city with a life of its own begins. Less culturally dynamic than Barcelona, less historic than Tarragona and less buzzy than Valencia it may be, but it has a good dose of all their qualities and on a far more speedily accessible scale.

The best way of mapping out the city is to take the clanking lift up from the Paseo Gomez to the **Castillo Santa Bàrbara** (summer 10am–8pm and winter 9am–7pm; you can park on the opposite side of the road from the lift). Today, after centuries of refortifying and bombardment, the castle is more impressive from below than from inside, but it is worth the trip up to the top for the urban panorama below. Immediately to the south lies the heart of the city, its broad Rambla neatly dissecting the scrambled old town from the more spacious 19th-century grid of streets and shady plazas while, to the north, a great arc of hotel and apartment skyscrapers curves round from the industrial port and a marina to a sweep of white beaches.

Ironically, it is right in the middle of the tourist sprawl, on a hillside above Albufereta beach, that the first Alicante grew up. The Greeks gave the Iberian settlement the name Akra Leuke (white

Alicante port

San Nicolás Cathedral, Alicante

peak), from which came the Roman name of Lucentum and the Arab or *valenciano* name of Alacant. The Carthaginians used it as a port, and Hannibal is said to have unloaded his famous war elephants here.

Finds from each culture, most notably the Iberian and Roman, are housed in the neoclassical **Diputación** (Avenida de la Estación 6; Monday to Friday 9am–2pm). The museum is only a 20-minute walk from the castle, heading along the **Explanada** and up through the graceful **Plaza Gabriel Miró**. In summer, stop off on the way at **Peret's** legendary seafront kiosk to grab a *horchata* (tiger-nut milk), a thirst-quenching drink in which locals like to dunk slabs of almond cake and sponge fingers.

The stroll back towards the old town through the small shopping street running off around the wonderful Modernist central market (newly restored) takes you past small shops selling everything from *paella* pans to traditional *alpargatas* or cut-price shoes sold direct from the factory. Walk past the 19th-century theatre – worth a peek inside – down the busy Rambla and across into **Calle San Isidro** to arrive at **San Nicolás**, the town's 17th-century cathedral. It is modest in scale and ornament by the standards of Spanish baroque because it was built as a collegiate church. Inside, do not miss the earlier Gothic cloister where a fountain trickles among ornamental oranges.

A stone's throw beyond is the 18th-century *ayuntamiento* housed in the old **Casa Consistorial**, with stunning reliefs both back and front by Juan Batista Borja, who also carved the Cathedral door. The first step is used as sea level for all altitude measurements made in Spain. The plaza's finest moment comes every July, on the last night of the *hogueras*, the city's biggest fiesta, when the mayor lights a trapeze-like fuse which sputters over the heads of the assembled crowd towards a massive wooden sculpture in the middle of the square. As it bursts into flame, the crowd erupts and the **Nit del Foc**, when nearly 100 such bonfires burn in sequence through the city, has officially begun.

All around the arcaded plaza and dotted around the old town are bars and restaurants that offer a *menú del día* (menu of the day, *see page 90*). **Nou Manoulin** – which is close to the bullring, a 10-minute walk away – is a cut above the rest, with an excellent cellar. It is worth the extra distance if you want to linger over a good meal. **Playa del Postiguet** is a good spot for an afternoon's sunbathing out of season, but when the crowds thicken you may prefer to drive past San Juan to **Cabo de Huertas**, a rocky oasis about 20 minutes away.

In the early evening, return to the old town, walking up the pedestrianised **Calle Mayor** – the city's main shopping street until the 19th century and still bustling today – to explore the **Barrio Santa Cruz**, originally the Moorish part of town and now the most atmospheric in a rakishly down-at-heel way. Doves flutter around the gargoyle and cherub-laden facade of **Santa María** church, which was built over the main mosque. Open briefly for evening mass around 6pm, the church is impossible to miss.

Next door is the **Museo de la Asegurada** (Pl. de Santa María; Tuesday to Saturday 10.30am–1.30pm and 6–9pm; October to April 10am–1pm and 5–8pm), an excellent contemporary art collection left to the city by abstract painter Eusebio Sempere. The works, unrelated except by personal taste, track international Modernism from Kandinsky to Christo, and represent all the great Spanish names of the twentieth century.

Behind the church and museum, small whitewashed houses noisy with early evening gossip and children's street games wind along and around the base of the castle's mound. In the **Calle San Raphael** there are several small café-bars where you can muster your strength before joining the evening *paseo* along the seafront Explanada. This is a quite different world from the Barrio de Santa Cruz, only a few hundred yards away. The wedding-cakey, bourgeois skyline is broken by a monstrous skyscraper of a hotel, horribly symbolic of the impact of tourism on this coast. Wander along under the shade of the huge fig trees, past the municipal bandstand and parents bouncing cologne-soaked children on their knees, to the Modernist fish market now restored as an exhibition centre. Close by is **Dársena**, where you can eat over 50 types of rice looking out over the port (*see page 90*).

Night time in Alicante is never dull. Depending on your tastes there is plenty of action in the bars of the Barrio Santa Cruz or the discos of San Juan (*see page 81*). If you are a real club enthusiast, Benidorm is not far away.

Above: La Explanada; night life
Right: Midsummer 'hogueras' festival, Alicante

DAY 5

The Segura Valley: Calasparra to Guardamar

A drive down the River Segura to Murcia city (allow 4 hours); then through the flatter lower valley past historic Orihuela to Guardamar and the sea (allow 3 hours). *See map on pages 26–7.*

Following rivers is one of the best ways of exploring Spain. The **Segura** is no exception. Rising high in the sierras of Jaen, it slows to a glassy snake by the time it reaches Murcia city. But behind that deceptive quietness, it is an immensely powerful river, irrigating a lush swathe of green that cuts through sierras and plains, villages and towns, narrowing and widening as it goes until it runs down to the coast through a sea of green fields.

River scene in inland Murcia

Join the river at **Calasparra**, which has been famous for its rice fields ever since the time of Philip V. At this point the water is very clean, rushing through a deep canyon that can be reached off the road along the left bank to **Cieza**. Take the first right after the cement works and drive up to the ruined farmhouse, where you can park and walk down to the dam (*presa*). There is also a place to swim here, but be careful, however: below the dam the water is extremely dangerous.

For the drive down to Cieza, double back to Calasparra and take the picturesque road along the right bank, passing a reservoir and pine forests before dropping down to the river and the lush *huerta* for the first time.

You come into Cieza over the old bridge; follow the signs out of town for **Abarán**. Here the valley suddenly narrows into the dramatically beautiful valley of **Ricote**, the road dipping and curving past plum and peach orchards, with the silhouette of Cieza castle perched above. These orchards are largely new, planted since the

Citrus groves, Ojós

small dam at Ojós allowed irrigation some 12 years ago. But the citrus groves further down, at **Blanca** and **Ojós**, standing out against the mountainsides like an oasis in the desert, recreate a sense of Muslim Spain. This is not merely poetic licence. The Moors first started irrigating the area in the 8th century, and they stayed here until 1611. Their imprint is all around you: in the walled paths running between the groves, in the occasional disused water wheels at the side of the river – which were replaced by electric pumps a mere 20 years ago – and in their double system of 'live' and 'dead' water, taking it from the river and then back again.

The **Vega Alta** – or upper river plain – ends in style at **Archena**, where 19th-century hotels stand over the thermal baths just outside town. Both the swimming pool in the sub-tropical gardens – you pay at the office – and the bar give a wonderful taste of Belle Epoque elegance. This section of the drive, from Calasparra to Archena, should take 2½ hours at an easy pace, not allowing for stops.

The road runs from here towards the small group of villages in the original Murcian *huerta*, or market garden, which was planted by the Romans and then extended by the Arabs. Since the middle of the 19th century it has steadily expanded, and now produces more lemons than any other region in Europe – as well as oranges, peppers, garlic and three crops a year of traditional market garden vegetables and fruit. Inevitably, preserving factories soon moved in – their 19th-century chimneys still break the skyline at **Molina de Segura** – and today, with the size of the *huerta* doubling again in the last 10 years, straggling agribusiness calls the tune. The river itself has coped, but only at the cost of bad contamination.

Nonetheless, there are interesting reminders of past times: at **Javalí Nuevo**, the small 10th-century *contraparada*, which still stands in the river, and, at **Alcantarilla**, one of the few working *norias* or Arab water wheels. It stands in the garden of the **Museo de la Huerta** (Ctra de Alcantarilla, by Alcantarilla turning; look for the water wheel on your right; Tuesday to Saturday 10am–7pm). The displays of tools, costumes, ceramics, woodcarving and the reconstructed *barraca*,

Murcia Cathedral

or cane and adobe cottage, describe a way of life that has now largely disappeared. All that remains are a few words of the local dialect, *panocho*, the dances and songs of the spring fiestas and the local cooking, which you can try next door for lunch at the **Mesón de la Huerta** (*see page 90*).

Guardamar

The drive from here into **Murcia city** should take half an hour, allowing for the traffic, and is largely suburban. In the centre, however, after crossing over the **Puente Viejo**, you can park and stroll along the river bank, taking in the **Cathedral** and the converted **mill** just below the bridge (C. de los Molinos, Monday to Saturday 11am–2pm and 6–9pm). For more on Murcia, *see page 75*.

From here, drive south along the road marked for the **Santuario de Fuensanta**, then turn to follow the right bank of the river, invisible behind rustling fields of sweet corn, sugarcane, cotton and newer tropical fruits or flowers. The road runs through scattered modern houses that are often flooded. From **Alquerías** to **Beniet**, you can follow a small farm road between the orchards. Shortly afterwards, at **Desamparados**, there is an excellent small **Museo Etnológico** (Monday to Friday 10.30am–1.30pm and 4.30–6.30pm, mornings only on Saturday; key in bookshop) with interesting displays of old work tools, furniture, photographs, religious objects and the like.

If you drive up to the sanctuary at **Orihuela** there is a wonderful view over the sea of mottled greens on the valley floor. Do not miss Orihuela's old centre while you are here (Orihuela is described in more detail in the itinerary opposite). Take the road down the right bank to Bigastro and **Jacarilla**, where there is a lovely garden laid out around the country house of the **Marqueses de Fontalbán** (open 9am–1pm and 5–6pm or sunset), then cross the river to **Callosa**, which has a fine Gothic and Renaissance church. The villages which follow between here and Guardamar were largely destroyed in the earthquake of 1829 and have an almost provisional feel to them. (Allow 2½ hours for the drive from Murcia to Guardamar, including detours.)

Guardamar itself keeps the feel of an old-fashioned river town, partly because the value of land has stopped tourism taking over and partly because it has a long history guarding the mouth of the river (an Iberian sculpture like the Dama de Elche was recently found here and is now in the Alicante museum). After crossing the iron bridge on the way into town, take the track immediately to the left, which will take you along the river – recently widened and deepened – down to the small quay at the mouth of the river. Here, the salt and fresh water meet and, further round, on the beach where there are 19th-century cottages, you will find the fishermen's boats and nets.

The same road loops on round to take you back towards town, through pines and close to a site where a 10th-century Muslim monastery and Phoenician wall have been unearthed from the sand. In town itself, there are a number of fish restaurants; the local *langostinos* are now almost impossibly expensive, but there are excellent rice dishes and *caldero*.

DAY 6

Orihuela and Lorca

Orihuela is a 30–40 minute drive from either Murcia or Alicante. You need a long morning to see its old centre. Lorca (a one hour's drive away) takes 2–3 hours. *See map on pages 26–7.*

Orihuela and Lorca belong to that peculiarly Spanish breed of historic towns in which everyday life ticks over, apparently unaware, against a backdrop of stunning architecture. Buildings crumble away. Opening times are maddeningly erratic. But it is this very lack of self-consciousness, the way in which tourism plays second fiddle to local life, that gives these towns such resonance.

Orihuela's (Oriola's) old quarter runs around the left bank of the river under the prow of the sierra. The aged buff-stone provincial shops and poor backstreets, crumbling palaces and the glassy river make the backdrop to the monumental centre.

Cathedral, Orihuela

The town's credentials explain its rich heritage: independent capital in the 8th century; launching pad for Ferdinand and Isabella's final assault on Granada; wealthy Renaissance university and cathedral city; commercial focus of the fertile lower Segura valley. Its political power faded only in the early 19th century, when Alicante took over as regional capital and five of its monasteries were dissolved. Today, despite its fame as the birthplace of Lorca's friend, Miguel Hernández, self-taught radical poet, it remains a deeply conservative *castellano*-speaking town, looking more to the past than the future.

There is space here to describe only a few highlights. One is the **Colegio de Santo Domingo** (Monday to Friday 10am–1pm; church 8–9pm) on the edge of town – turn immediately right under the arched **Puerta de Crevillente** (called the angels' gate) at the end of the palm forest. The graceful proportions of its cloistered patios spell out its importance, first as a convent and later as a university (1610–1824). Now it is a private school run by the bishopric. You are unlikely to gain access to the church, but don't miss the tiled frieze in the former refectory, one of the best in the region, or the panelled and coffered main staircase. The birthplace of Miguel Hernández is nearby in Calle Miguel Hernández (Monday to Friday 10.30am–1.30pm and 4.30–6.30pm, morning only on Saturday).

Another highlight is the shadowy **Cathedral**, an inspired small-scale patchwork of styles from Romanesque and Catalan Gothic to baroque. Below the vaulting, defined by spiral ribs, there is fine Renaissance ironwork, a rich 17th-century carved choir, an ornate baroque organ and, in the sacristy, Velázquez's wonderful *Temptation of Saint Thomas*. This is only the most famous among many interesting, if often unidentified, paintings in the museum (Monday to Friday 10.30am–1pm and 4–6pm, voluntary contribution). There are many other curiosities too, such as the 16th-century brass Virgen del Cabildo, made for economy with two detachable heads and pairs of hands to change her character. Opposite the Cathedral, on the river itself, stands the 17th-century **Palacio Episcopal**, with its very fine cloister.

Further along the river stands the church of **Santas Justa** and **Rufina**, its gargoyled clock tower marking the southern boundary of Catalan Gothic. Beyond the Renaissance **town hall** and the **Palacio**

Lorca's castle.

Baroque splendour in Lorca

Rubalcalba, where the tourist office and a good bar are located, is the **Church of Santiago** (Monday to Saturday 10am–12.30pm and 5–7pm), its carved Isabelline portal bearing the yolk and arrows of the Catholic kings. Inside, the Gothic austerity is broken by rich altarpieces by Salzillo, the Murcian sculptor whose lyrical realism has come to define Spanish baroque. More of his work can be viewed in the **Iglesia de la Merced**, where the town's *pasos*, processional sculptures for Holy Week, are kept (Monday to Friday 10.30am–1.30pm and 4–6pm, Saturday 10.30am–1.30pm).

The best central eating place is **Los Barriles**, Calle Sal 1, tel: 966 530 6498. Here there is a wonderful combination of the rice so typical of Alicante and vegetables of the Murcian *huerta.*

Like Orihuela, **Lorca** is more than the sum of its parts. The approach along the dusty main road to Andalucia through one of the most arid regions of Spain is hardly encouraging. But the old town, running down a gentle slope, is another world, quietly faded in some parts, crumbling away or abandoned in others. It grew up as a Roman highway stop on the Vía Heraklia linking the mines of Jaen to the port of Cartagena, and then became a strongly defended frontier city between Moorish *taifas*. Hence its oldest buildings are civic rather than religious: a Roman milestone, the castle keep and a medieval city gate.

But, as in Orihuela, the overall feel is Renaissance and baroque, the result of a building splurge after the reconquered town had been slowly repopulated by Catalans and Aragonese. You will find turrets, elaborate shields, cornices and carved doorways decorating Italianate aristocratic houses, the granary and the town hall on the central **Plaza de España**. **San Patricio**, the largest of the town's churches – so called because Alfonso X took the town from the Moors on St Patrick's day – looms up in lofty splendour behind its baroque facade. It was stripped of much decorative detail in the Civil War, but there are still a number of fine 17th-century paintings, including a black Christ, hanging among the motley collection. Among the town's other 10 churches, **San Francisco** is particularly worth a look (most are not left open during the day).

Over the last few years, the old town has undergone a major overhaul intended to inject new life into it. Houses are being restored with their traditional balconies and *palominas*, or outside hanging larders. It has also become one of the main crafts centres of Spain, with an excellent **Centro Regional de Artesanía** built on **Calle Lopez de Gisbert**, next to the **Iglesia San Mateo** (Tuesday to

Friday 10am–2pm and 4.30–7.30pm, Saturday morning only). Here you can examine the best selection of local crafts in the region, most notably the famed embroidered wool and silk used to dress the figures of the Semana Santa processions. There is also a good range of the ceramics and pottery – clearly Moorish influenced – of the towns of the Sierra de Espuña.

Three small museums, one archaeological (Palacio del Maqués del Esquilache, Tuesday to Friday 10am–2pm and 6–8pm, weekends 11am–2pm) and the other two devoted to the town's embroidery, opened in 1991. For the time being though, there is more life in the evening either in the lower part of town, where there are bars and ice cream shops, or down by the river.

DAY 7

The Southern Coast: Cartagena to Alicante

The coast road from Cartagena to Alicante goes through mining country, to Calblanque beach, with lunch at Cabo de Palos (1 hour's drive); in the afternoon, up past Guardamar to Santa Pola (1¾ hours' drive) and Tabarca island, reached by boat. *See map on pages 26–7.*

The road south from Alicante cuts through flat, luminous landscape past an open shoreline which at first sight appears featureless. Only dusty palms and new apartment blocks seem to break the long stretches of sand. Closer inspection, however, reveals much of interest: the fortified island and marine nature reserve at Santa Pola; a string of saltpans; one of the most unspoiled beaches of the coast, and finally, Cartagena, with its curious combination of ancient history and modern industrial wealth (*for details see page 77*).

If you don't plan to come back it is worth visiting the main museums and seeing some of the Modernist architecture in

Alicante

The face of modern Alicante

the city. If you are really looking for a quiet day without diving into a big city, skip Cartagena and take the road to **La Unión**, which grew out of two 19th-century mining villages and has a couple of fine Modernist buildings – the **Antiguo Mercado Publico** and **Casa del Piñón**. It is known for one of Spain's best flamenco festivals, based on the mining songs, a local form of flamenco that grew with the arrival of Andalucian immigrant workers.

From here, turn off into the valley of **Portman**. Curiously reminiscent of the Welsh hills, littered with old-fashioned mining machinery, it is now an ecological disaster, the bay silted up from mining refuse and its jetty landlocked by a skin of mineral residue. Dumping was finally banned in 1990 and attempts are now being made to replant the shoreline, but it will take centuries for the ecological balance to establish itself again. In the meantime, the valley has a mournful beauty, its industrial bleakness set against a rugged shoreline.

The valley road hooks up to join the main road to **Cabo de Palos**, passing a dreadful up-market villa estate on the way. So far, however, most of this stretch of coastline has avoided development, keeping a gloriously unspoiled spread of empty sandy and rocky bays at **Calblanque**. To reach it, soon after passing through Los Velones, turn right down a marked track. Calblanque is protected as part of a *parque natural*, and its waters are limpid and clear, with wonderful snorkelling and sub-aqua diving further around, off the point of the **Cabo** and the **Islas Hormigas**. How long the *parque* will resist the threat of development is unclear – so far it has been kept at bay by the strength of local opinion – but for the time being, it remains one of the most unspoiled pockets of the Mediterranean coast.

At weekends, locals stream out past here to eat fish at **Cabo de Palos**, a small fishing port with a lighthouse and old-fashioned villas dotted around it. In the restaurants along the seafront (*see page 91*) are platefuls of *caldero*, the local fishermen's meal of rice cooked in stock followed by a plateful of fish or,

Santa Pola; port and Tabarca ferry

more expensive, fish baked in a salt crust. The small bay, with its views of the fishing boats bobbing in the port, makes the perfect setting for a relaxed and fortifying lunch.

By comparison with Calblanque, there is nothing of great scenic beauty left around the **Mar Menor**, the small inland sea formed by a sand bar that has built up over thousands of years. Twenty years ago, when tourist promotion began under the slogan 'A Paradise between Two Seas', the white dunes of the **Manga**, as the sand bar is called, were as empty as a desert, and the unique flora and fauna based on the very salty and warm sheltered waters flourished.

Today, however, the shimmering skyline created by the hotels is more aptly compared to Miami, and the villages of the inland shore are geared to family tourism and water sports. But, thankfully, the plans of developers to open up a road onto the Manga from the north were recently blocked and the little that is left as a *parque natural* remains protected.

For emptier beaches and a refreshing quick afternoon swim, drive on either to the far end of **Dehesa de Campoamor**, where rusty cliffs drop down to small and often empty coves – rapidly being surrounded by indiscriminate building – or to **Guardamar del Segura** (about 1½ hour's drive from Cabo de Palos) and its windswept beach by the river's mouth. Nearby, it has a small but interesting archaeological site – a series of mosques being unearthed from a thick blanket of sand – and a huge pine grove planted to stop the dunes overwhelming the village (*see pages 44–5*).

Beyond that, the road runs past salt pans to **Santa Pola**, the most interesting of the southern resorts once you have made it to the seafront. Next to the port, home to the largest deep sea and coastal fleet of the Mediterranean, you can catch a boat to **Tabarca** (*for sailings see page 112*), the main island of a small archipelago in the bay, which Charles III fortified and settled with Genoese prisoners in the 18th century. The walled town now looks like a grandiose folly, the unfinished church and entrance arch ridiculously oversized next to the squat fishing shacks and dusty roads. On the other half of the island you will find the old lighthouse and solar station that generates the island's electricity (a walk around the island takes about 1½ hours).

Only 100 or so people live on the island now, following a seasonal double life: in winter, they tend to work on the fishing boats and in summer, in the *chiringuitos*, or beach restaurants. The visitors flood in here for various reasons, some simply for the refreshing breeziness of the beaches and the *caldero* in the restaurants, others to do some serious snorkelling or sub-aqua diving, since the waters around the island have some of the most interesting submarine life off the Costa Blanca. Ecologists consider the marine reserve surrounding the archipelago a model of its type, which will hopefully be replicated elsewhere along the shore to regenerate the dying underwater ecosystem.

You can stay on the island until sunset, when it is at its emptiest and most beautiful, or return to the mainland in time for the fish market at 5pm and to see the aquarium and clinic for sick turtles in the Plaza Francisco Fernández Ordoñez (Tuesday to Sunday 11am–1.30pm and 4–8pm; holidays, 11am–1.30pm). Afterwards, head for one of the busy fish restaurants. The most interesting local dish is the *gazpacho de pescado*, a marine adaptation of the inland game stews, but all the usual rices and *caldero* are excellent too. And, if you have the energy and inclination, in summer Santa Pola also has a good crop of seasonal discotheques where you can frolic the night away (*see page 83*).

Isla de Tabarca

1. The Albufera

It is 1½ hours by motorway from Alicante to the marshy inland lagoon of the Albufera, famous for its migratory bird life, rice fields and paella restaurants. *See map on page 24.*

The freshwater lagoon of the **Albufera** is only a stone's throw from Valencia city, but it remains one of Spain's most distinctive rural landscapes – a watery patchwork of river fields, thatched *barracas*, marshland and dunes, now protected as a *parque natural* for the value of its aquatic wildlife, which includes some 250 bird species. The lagoon itself was once a vast lake – its name means 'small sea' in Arabic – but over the centuries it has shrunk to a tenth of its original size as the shallows have silted up and the edges filled in to plant rice. As you come from the south, the road past **Cullera** and **Sueca** (N332) takes you through the paddy fields. The best lookout point is the Monte de los Santos, where the tiny church is dedicated to the rice saints Adón and Senen (turn off at Sueca).

El Palmar is the oldest of the four lake villages. Built on an islet of reclaimed land in the 19th century, it has kept its canals, landing quay and *barraca* splashed with ochre and cobalt. It was James I who, after the Reconquest, granted the local people the right to fish the lagoon and set up the Tribunal de Aguas to settle disputes. Seven centuries later, it still meets on the steps of Valencia's Cathedral every Thursday morning. From this time, too, date the *comunidades*, societies to which the fishermen belong, and the *albuferencs*, the long, flat-bottomed punts used for fishing and travelling around the rice paddies. Quaintly archaic as it may all sound, fishing here has a firmly modern base in the export market for the lakes' fat grey mullet (*llissas*) and eels (*anquilas*).

Today the *albuferencs* and other small fishing boats are motorised and also ferry around tourists. They can be hired at **El Palmar** or **El Saler** and are well worth the money, since the lake is mesmerisingly beautiful whether its surface is a trembling blue in the heat of the summer sun, mournfully grey-green in winter or, best of all, saturated with colour at sunset. This is the ideal time to be out on the water with a pair of binoculars to enjoy the bird life: egrets, widgeon, herons and various kinds of grebes.

Walking is also a good way to build up an appetite. *Paella* originated as a poor country dish based on the ingredients to hand – rice, snails, fresh green and dried white beans, and rabbit or other game in winter, cooked over a wood fire. The version served at **Racó de l'Olla** (*see page 92*) is true to the original – or try the cheaper restaurants in **Catarroja**, the least touristy of the villages.

2. Xàtiva and Gandía: the Land of the Borjas

Allow 40 minutes' drive from the coast to reach Xàtiva, home town of the Borgias, and another 2–3 hours to look around; in the afternoon, Gandía gives the option of town or beach. *See map on page 24.*

The history of the Borgias (or Borjas), is usually thought of as Italian because Rome was the base of their nepotism, power politics and sexual intrigues. From there Alfonso de Borgia, Pope Calixto III, orchestrated the 15th-century campaign against the Turks, his nephew Alexander VI carved up the New World between the Spanish and Portuguese and his son, Caesar, on whom Machiavelli modelled *The Prince*, conspired to have his brother murdered.

But the Borgias, properly spelt Borjas, were of Spanish blood, with their family home in the Valencian hill town of **Xàtiva (Játiva** in *castellano*) and their aristocratic base, bought in the 15th century, in the nearby duchy of Gandía.

Main Cathedral, Xàtiva

Xàtiva, a pleasant 40-minute drive back from the coast, is the more interesting of the two towns. Try to visit it on market day (Tuesday or Thursday); otherwise, make sure you come in the morning when the **museum** is open (15 June to 15 September, Tuesday to Friday 11am–2pm and 4–6pm, Saturday and Sunday 11am–2pm; otherwise 9am–2.30pm). Its small but interesting collection traces the town's growth from Roman *castrum* (fortress), Visigothic bishopric and cultivated Arab town – thought to be one of the first places where paper was made in Europe – to royal city from the 14th to the 17th centuries. The collection includes a unique Romanesque font, and paintings by José Ribera (d.1591), nicknamed El Spagnaletto, yet another famous native son who made his name in Italy – his paintings are nonetheless considered part of the Spanish School because they had such a great influence. To make sure you catch everything of interest in the old town, follow the tourist office's numbered walking route, which takes you past old palaces, noble houses – including Alexander VI's birthplace – fountains and churches to **La Seo**, the huge collegiate church, which was sacked in the Civil War (Monday to Saturday 9–10.45am and 6.30–8.30pm, Sunday 9am–1.30pm). On the top of the hill above are the **ruins** of the Roman to medieval city and castle, destroyed by Philip III in revenge for Xàtiva's siding against him in the War of Succession (Tuesday to Sunday 10am–2pm and 4.30–7pm or 3.30–6pm in winter; allow an hour), and, just below that, the 13th-century church of **San Felix**, its doorway built with columns from the Roman Temple on the same site (open 10am–1pm and 4–7pm or 3–6pm in winter). For lunch, *see page 92*.

Siesta, Xàtiva

Gandía cannot compare with Xàtiva for atmosphere or monumental wealth, but it does have the **collegiate church** built in the time of of Calixtus III (Monday to Saturday 9am–noon and 7–8pm) and the sumptuous 16th- to 18th-century former palace of the Borjas, the **Palacio de Santo Duque** (too rich for some tastes; guided tours 11am, noon, 5pm, 6pm). It was turned into Spain's first Jesuit college by the fourth duke, Francisco Borja. Abandoning his ancestors' examples, he turned his back on earthly wealth after the death of his wife, joined the Jesuits and became the Superior of the order. The palace has an outstanding allegorical tiled floor. Nearby is a good cake-shop, **Dolços Toni**, C. Pares Jesuits 5, where you can recover from so much religiosity.

3. Valley and Sierras: Pego and Agres

The inland valley between Pego and Agres (total 1½ hours' drive without stopping) can be seen in a day. *See map on page 24.*

Nowhere is the contrast between the modernity of the coast and the traditional way of life inland so marked as it is in the **Vall de Gallinera** and the **Vall de Agres**, with their quiet agricultural villages, Moorish imprint and surrounding sierras. To get a proper feel of them, you need to allow two to three days; plan to travel on foot as well as by car. The springboard for both is **Pego**, now a bustling small town, which has lost its rice fields but keeps an agricultural feel (and the large front doors through which tractors can pass). If you get there early enough (9–10am), you will be able to see the fine 15th-century *retablo* of the pregnant **Virgen de la Esperanza** in the parish church.

From Pego, take the road to **Planes** (marked for **Muro de Alcoy** or **Muro del Comtat**) into the **Vall de Gallinera**. The traces of the converted Moors who stayed after the Reconquest quickly show themselves: the terracing of the steeply banked hillsides, and then, after the road has run through a spectacular gorge, the Arabic names and layout of the old *alquerías*, or hamlets. Some of the more isolated villages – Alcalà de la Jovada, for example – even have deserted, dry-stone *morisco* ruins still standing. The area became a stronghold for rebellion: one revolt, led by the charismatic Al-Azraq, lasted from 1258–75; another was a dramatic last stand against expulsion in 1609 by 15,000 *moriscos*. Outnumbered, they eventually surrendered and were deported the following spring.

Just before you reach Planes, a track hairpinning down to the right, signed for the **Barranc del' Encanta** – literally the 'enchanted ravine' – leads to a wonderful blue swimming hole fed by a waterfall. From here you can walk along the valley floor between olive and citrus groves, or drive on up to the ruined castle at **Lorcha**. **Planes** itself, perched on a small hill below a ruined 12th-century castle,

View from Agres to the Sierra de la Filosa

Colourful river bed, Pego

has kept its medieval shape, a 17th-century aqueduct built for a long defunct distillery, the oldest fiesta in the province (*see page 103*) and a string of bars along the main road. At the next village, **Benimarfull**, the **Cooperativa San Jaime** serves excellent grilled chops and sausages.

It is only half-an-hour's drive from here to **Agres**, tucked into the side of its quiet valley. The **Pensión Mariola** (*see page 113*) in the village makes a good base for a quiet night or two, with excellent walking country round about. Up on the **Sierra de Mariola**, there are medieval snow-wells in which ice was made for the summer, prehistoric caves and a large number of wild herbs (take the forest path up past the sanctuary, which is also worth a look). Down in the valley, a path leads along various stretches of the river and there is an old *balneario* or spa. A short drive on up the valley will also bring you to **Bocairent**, a quiet market town with a picturesque medieval quarter.

After all this, returning to the coast comes as a shock. The villa developments overlooking Pego seem to stand out more brutally than before and one is left wondering how long the valleys can resist development.

4. A Night on the Town in Benidorm

You'll need your own car or a taxi from the old town to the clubs off Levante beach. *See map on page 24.*

It is easy to knock **Benidorm** – particularly when you have never set eyes on it. Most people who have actually deigned to go there will admit that, even for those who don't like package tourism, there is a fascination in the style with which Benidorm does it. In this sense, it is rather like Las Vegas: a cultural phenomenon of our times. The largest resort in the world, a huge fun factory – it must be seen to be believed. And, quite apart from all this, its nightlife has something to offer everyone, from a gay acid-house kid to an 80-year-old granny.

Arrive at sundown as the three miles of white sand are emptying, and you will be in time to catch the evening *paseo*. Follow the signs through the mini-skyscrapers to the **Playa** (or **Platja**) **de Levante** (if you are in a car, leave it in the underground park off **Avda de L'Aigüera**) and stroll along the front, past the tea cafés where old-age pensioners happily tango away winter afternoons (many a second romance is formed here). Despite all the foreigners, the *paseo* is also a wonderful cross-section of old and new Spain:

mini-skirted girls twice the height of their grandmothers, old men in their berets, women gesticulating with their fans.

The three miles of white sand on which Benidorm has grown wealthy are an object lesson in how beaches can be kept clean if you really try. An army of rubbish collectors move in at dusk, and after midnight dumper trucks start the long job of sifting out cigarette butts and oxygenating the sand. Out in the bay, a filter cleans and monitors the water. Beach bars are banned. Hence, despite the 45,000 people who squeeze onto the twin beaches at the height of the season, the beaches have been declared among the eight cleanest beaches in the world in a survey by an ecological group.

Once it is dark, walk back to **L'Aigüera** (daylight–10pm; July–September to 1am), a post-Modernist park designed by controversial Catalan architect Ricardo Bofill. Among the various schemes to move Benidorm up-market, this is the most spectacular and imaginative, and it has an added interest as the first major piece of public architecture in one of the coastal resorts. Built along a dried-up river valley, its central avenue runs up through sweeping classical perspectives which are transformed at night by blue and white neon lighting. The new town hall in front of the park – also designed by Bofill – is a grandiose testament to the profits of tourism.

L'Aigüera Park, Benidorm

Eating possibilities also break the mould, especially now that so many Spanish are coming here. For specific addresses, see *Dining Experiences* – or simply pick up a snack in the old town. Take your time over your meal because the action in the clubs doesn't start until after midnight – and well after that, in the places that are patronised by the local Spanish population.

There are two main centres of nightlife. The first is the old town, where you will find the more local bars, ice cream parlours and *horchaterías* as well as the gay clubs, recognised by music and lights behind plain facades. As everywhere in Spain, these usually have a relaxed mixed clientele. The other main area is new Benidorm, at the far end of the **Levante beach**, where **Penelope**, the biggest disco, and its rivals are clustered together. More interesting in this zone are **Triana**, a late-night *sevillanas* club, **Arte** and **L'Anouer**, up-market bars, or **Star Garden**, the ultimate discotheques (see *Nightlife, page 82*).

If you can stick the pace and make it right through the night, then finish off with an early morning cup of hot chocolate – one of the best you will ever have – at Buana, or one of the other bars along the main road in **Villa joyosa (La Vila Joiosa)**, before finally dropping into bed or falling asleep on the beach.

5. Early Evening in the Guadalest Valley

Allow 45 minutes to Guadalest from the turn-off behind Benidorm, and the same to Altea la Vieja for dinner. *See map on page 24.*

The **Guadalest valley** is one of the most photogenic of Alicante province's landscapes, with tall peaks and hill villages above sub-tropical green valleys.

For an evening trip in summer, start around 7.30 or 8pm in **Polop de la Marina**, a dozy village with the tall mountain of **Ponoch** looming above it on one side. The main tourist sight here is the Font Els Zorros, a modern extension of the old water fountain with 221 spouts. From here the village streets slope steeply up towards the deserted cemetery, built on the site of the **ruined castle**. There are fine views over the lush, sub-tropical valley floor below and the surrounding peaks, often backed by swirling clouds. The road continues to Callosa, where you could take in a swim at the Fonts de Algar (*see page 32*).

At Callosa, take the turning for **Benimantell**, which runs through almond and olive groves and gives you the best first view of the village of **Guadalest**, its castle and bell tower precariously balanced on fangs of rock rearing up from the valley. It was one of a dense network of Muslim castles which collected taxes and kept an eye on the scattered rural hamlets in these northern valleys. Now, the silhouette and view from the top of the castle are, in truth, its

Guadalest

8. A Picnic at Tibi Reservoir

A visit to a 16th-century dam and reservoir, 50-minutes drive inland from Alicante. Wear sensible shoes. *See map on page 25.*

Tibi village has little or nothing to make it stand out from countless others in the inland sierras of Alicante: a few shops and bars, a village cooperative and a shady main street. What makes it worth visiting are its reservoir and dam, built over 14 years at the end of the 16th century (1580–94) to irrigate the Alicante *huerta*, and still functioning today.

The reservoir and dam are most easily reached off the road from Alicante to Castalla. Coming from Alicante, turn right down an unmarked road into a small housing development called the **Urbanización Maigmó**, about 100 metres after a garage and 200 metres before the turn-off to **Agost** (if you get lost, ask at the garage for the *embalse*). Take the second road on the right, which is signposted, and follow it round, then keep straight all the way over four small junctions, until you come to a farm. Here the road swings right and down towards the reservoir until, after a total of 5km (3 miles), it reaches the clearing for parking. Leave the car here and proceed on foot.

Tibi Dam

There is a choice of two approaches to the dam, one a short cut up the slope to your left, which brings you straight out on top of the dam; the other route, more spectacular – but not advisable for children or, for that matter, those without a head for heights – leading down a path to the right and so to a small bridge with a plaque to Charles IV, from where you get the first complete view of the dam, directly upstream, built between a narrow gorge.

Although its overall dimensions are nothing like those of many modern dams, the severe curved wall, making brilliant use of the natural geography, is a magnificent sight when you stand below it, listening to the eerie sound effects of the water and air eddying within and watching the overflow splash down from above, down onto the rocks below.

A dizzying climb of over 100 steps cut into the rock, with only a crumbling rail to hold, takes you up to the top of the dam. Into its worn blocks of stone is set a plaque commemorating its refurbishment in 1794. This is a wonderful place to have a picnic, looking out onto the reservoir on one side and down the wall of the dam on the other.

9. The Cave of Canalobre

A 45-minute drive into the hills from Alicante to the Cuevas de Canalobre; it is advisable to go late or at lunchtime to avoid the crowds. *See map on page 25.*

Discovered by the Moors around 12 centuries ago, the vast stalagmite-filled cave of **Canalobre**, 3km (1.8 miles) from the village of **Busot** and 26km (16 miles) from Alicante, has seen various reincarnations over the centuries. Wartime refuge, religious shrine and, aircraft-engine factory during the Civil War, it has now been converted into a perfect monument of our own age: a tourist attraction, complete with piped music echoing around the dripping walls and fanciful names for rock formations (8am–7.40pm in summer and 11am–5.40pm in winter; admission charge). From a purist point of view it is disappointing, since there is little or no atmosphere and no information available on the geology or history, but it is highly popular, with some 50,000 people visiting the Cuevas every year.

Canalobre cave

This is a perfect destination for children. And even for adults, the proportions of the main cave – shaped like a tall chamber over 100m (328ft) high and filled by stalagmites and other rock formations – are impressive, especially when you first enter, looking down as if from the roof of a cathedral. Stairs (safely roped) lead around and through the stalagmites and stalagtites, the most spectacular of which are the huge candelabra after which the cave was named. Close by one of the largest are the broken remains of a Moorish column. If you ask and are interested, you may also be able to see the seismographic equipment kept here as part of the national network.

Few people would want to spend more than a quarter of an hour in the cave itself. But the landscape and views back to the coast through harsh, rocky countryside are spectacular and it would be easy to make a longer trip out of it, either by adding on a walk and picnic – take the bumpy, rutted track off to the right as you drive back down the hillside below the cave – or by going on to Jijona, Tibi and Agost.

Wine country on the road to Yecla

10. The Murcian Wine Country: Jumilla and Yecla

Allow 1 hour to reach Yecla from Alicante or 1¼ from Murcia city and 20 minutes on to Jumilla, where there is a good restaurant for lunch. *See map on pages 26–7.*

Where **Murcia** bulges north towards **La Mancha** and opens up into gentle sierras and plateaus, the landscape becomes reminiscent of the central *meseta* of nearby **Castile**. The horizons, wide and full of light, are sparsely populated and cut across by straight roads; the farming land is planted with wheat, olives and vines. Of the three, it is the vines which dominate today. **Yecla** is the larger of the two *denominaciones*. 'This good town of countrymen…' wrote the novelist Azorín in the early twentieth century, 'they love, but love the earth…and they have enormous faith, the faith of the early mystics…this is the old Spain, legendary, heroic.'

The legacy of the faith is a string of churches. Cutting up towards the old town along Calle Perales and San Francisco, you will pass three of them along the way: **San Roque** (with a wonderful *mudéjar* wooden ceiling), **San Francisco** (Renaissance to baroque) and, further up, the massive blue-domed **Iglesia de la Purísima**, which the town struggled and scraped to build for a whole century (*c*1750–1868). At the very top, on the **Plaza Mayor**, stand the mellow-stoned Renaissance **granary** and 19th-century **corn exchange**, and the Church of **San Salvador**, badly damaged but with its 16th-century pyramidal tower intact (in particular, check out the carved frieze of faces under the parapet).

The agricultural base of the town has disappeared now, replaced by furniture manufacturing which grew out of coopering. But the vineyards remain all-important. On the edge of town, at the massive **Cooperativa de la Purísima**, one of the largest in Spain, you can taste and buy the local reds, which vary between powerful table wines in the old style, with a lot of body and colour – sometimes called macho wines – and smoother, fruity blends adapted to modern drinking tastes, for which the harvest is brought forward to reduce the sugar content of the grapes.

The reds from neighbouring **Jumilla**, a 20-minute drive from Yecla, have been famed since Roman times. They are even more full-bodied (some are 16° strong), a result of intense summer heat and the age of the vines, which are the only Spanish and among the very few European vines not to have been damaged by phylloxera. On the way into town, at **La Alquería**, you will pass the co-operative of **San Isidro**, the town's largest *bodega*, which sells table wine from the barrel, bottled vintages matured in oak ('73, '80 and '81 are prime years), *vino rancio* matured in wood, sweet *mistela* and delicious local cheeses resembling mild young Manchegos. Of the half-dozen other *bodegas*, **Carcelen** has a small museum and lighter wines (8.30am–2pm and 5–8pm, Calle Murcia 102, tel: 968 780 418).

Jumilla is, quite apart from the fame of its wines, a charming small market town which has kept a stronger agricultural base than Yecla. It boasts the 16th-century monastery of **Santa Ana** (with an eccentric museum of curiosities brought by Franciscans from all over the world), a private house designed by Gaudí and, **Casa Sebastián**, one of a breed of restaurants which has now all but disappeared. It has crates of provisions stacked around the walls, hatches opening into the small kitchen and no written menu. But the lack of fuss is deceptive. Fina and Sebastián Bernal have decades of experience and it shows. Eat, drink from the ample cellar and enjoy (*see page 92*).

If you would like to extend the trip to a full day, you could go on to **Monóvar** and its surrounding wine villages (*see Option 12, page 71*), or drive into the **Sierra del Carche** or Llanos de Yecla, a reserve with rare birds of prey.

11. Frontier Territory: the Vinalopó Valley

Allow a leisurely day to see all the Vinalopó's castles, starting in Alicante, or turn back at Biar (Bihar) for a half-day trip. *See map on page 25.*

The broad valley floor of the **Vinalopó** has always been both a strategic route and frontier territory. Here, the cultures of the Bronze Age divided, the Carthaginians were defeated by the Romans, the Muslim kingdom of Murcia met its northern boundary and Castile battled with Aragon for over a century. Today, perched on rocky outcrops, stand medieval castles, silent markers of the old frontiers of Muslim and Christian.

Now that these castles have no military function, it is easy to forget their earlier political and military importance. As Philip V wrote in 1704, during the War of Spanish Succession, 'It is more important for me to keep Alicante than Valencia, because if Valencia were lost, which God forfend, it alone will be lost; but if Alicante were lost, both Valencia and Castile would be lost.'

Castalla

The castle of **Santa Bárbara** in **Alicante,** which was built first as a virtually impregnable tower in Muslim times, has had many later additions. Among its surviving elements, the most interesting are the 16th- and 17th-century additions modelled on the French Vauban system and the sheer scale of the walled area, which could garrison up to 40,000 men (*see details on page 38*).

From Alicante, take the road through **San Vicente de Raspeig** and **Aspe**, driving past almond trees and vineyards, to **Novelda** (about 40 minutes drive). Just beyond is the castle of **La Mola**, well known for its superb 12th-century triangular tower designed by Ibrahim of Tunis, a famous Arab military engineer. The tower stands above an eye-catching small Modernist sanctuary designed by Sala, a disciple of Gaudí. In the town itself, off the Placa d'Espanya, is a perfectly preserved **Casa Modernista** (9.30am–1.30pm and 4.30–6.30pm and Saturday 11am–2pm). It is then 15 minutes up the motorway to **Villena**, passing two more Hispano-Arabic castles: **Petrel** and **Sax**, the latter with an extraordinary setting, perched like an eagle's nest above the old town (the key is kept in the *ayuntamiento*). Both castles have been heavily restored.

For this reason, Villena's castle, **La Atalaya** (literally, the 'watchtower') is more impressive close up (it is left open – unlatch the studded door). Heavily fortified by the Almohades in the 12th century – their brick vaulting survives inside the superb keep – it became the centre of a powerful feudal state owing allegiance to Castile, controlling and protected by a string of smaller castles: **La Mola**, **Sax**, **Elda**, **Chinchilla** and **Almansa** (the last two in **Albacete** on the road to Madrid). In the 15th century it fell into the hands of

Castle in Sax

Fountain, Biar

the Pachecos, hugely powerful masters of the Order of Santiago, who built the thick double outer walls and the upper watchtowers of the keep. You can walk right around the walls, which took a bad battering in the War of Independence against the French: below the castle spreads the old town.

From Villena, you can take either of two routes. The longer option loops north to the town of **Bañeres (Bañyeres de la Mariola)**, which has a Gothic church and yet another Hispano-Arabic castle (11am–2pm and 4–8pm; the key is at C. Castillo 20), this time in Aragonese hands after the Reconquest. It looks out over **four provinces** – **Valencia**, **Murcia**, **Albacete** and **Alicante** – and also marks part of the dividing line between *castellano*- and *valenciano*-speaking territories. As a result, the local dialect often mixes its idioms.

Alternatively, if you have only the morning or afternoon, you can go straight to **Biar (Bihar)**, again on the Aragonese side of the old border. The prettiest of all these castle towns, its steeply banked old quarter rises sharply and you climb up long flights of steps to reach the castle. The scene of one of the hardest-fought battles in the Reconquest, it has the oldest surviving example of octagonal Almohade vaulting. Stop off in the **Plaça de le Constitució** below for a quick look at the church – a typical mix of styles, with Renaissance doorway and baroque frescoes over Gothic form.

The road on to Alicante will also take you past **Castalla**, where there are more castle ruins and a great restaurant (*see page 90*).

12. Monóvar and its Wine Villages

Monóvar is a 45-minutes drive from Alicante. Allow 2 hours to visit the town, and another 3 to explore the surrounding wine villages and to have lunch. *See map on page 25.*

Until the end of the 19th century, Monóvar's red wine was among the most sought-after in Europe. Transparent and slightly sweet, it was said to be an aphrodisiac – probably on account of its high alcohol content. It was also among the most expensive: in the late 19th century, at the height of its demand after French vineyards were destroyed by phylloxera, one shipload covered the building costs of the Casino in Monóvar three times over. But tastes in wine changed, the French vineyards were replanted and today the vineyards are little known.

This makes them all the more interesting to visit, since the wines are hard to find outside the region, the villages remain unspoiled and the *bodegas* are not over-commercialised. In summer they usually open in the morning only (9am–2pm); the rest of the year you can also taste and buy in the afternoon (4–7pm). From the coast, take the back road from Alicante via **Agost** (*see page 63*) and **Novelda**, which passes first through almond groves and then, after you have crossed under the motorway, into the limy vineyards. Trellised vines run in an unbroken sea until they rise, banked in hillside terraces, to meet the sierras looming in the background. The native Monastrel grapes are largely used for making red wine; Verdil for white.

Monóvar (Monóver) is small, but has a strong personality. The clock tower leans drunkenly at the top of the town and the church is missing one of its bell towers. There are other curiosities too: a wonderfully jumbled collection of local arts, crafts and work tools on display at the **Museo de Artes y Oficios** (by advance arrangement, tel: 96 547 0270); and the birthplace of **Azorín,** prolific essayist, novelist and politician of the generation of 1898 (Calle Salamanca 6, Monday to Friday 10am–2pm and 4–6pm, Saturday 11am–2pm).

Among the *bodegas*, **Salvador Poveda**, the biggest, is right in the centre of town (Calle Benjamín Palencia, open 7am–3pm). It is best known for its fragrant pudding wine, Fondillón, King Juan Carlos's favourite after-dinner tipple, which needs to be matured for 20 years (beware of cheap imitations), but also produces blood-coloured reds and excellent, delicate rosés. Their character comes from the local wine-making method, in which the rosé is fermented from must drawn off during a first light crushing of the grapes, and the red from a *doble pasta* in which the first batch of must and grapes is mixed with a second one in the same vat before fermentation. Another family *bodega* on the edge of town, **Primitivo Quiles**, produces similar wines and delicious vermouth.

From Monóvar, you can continue on a short circular route which takes you around the **Sierra de Reclot** and through the other wine

villages – **Hondón** (where a cooper still works), **Mañar**, **Culebrón**, **Pinoso**, **Algueña** and **La Romana**. All these villages are known for their earthy country cooking, especially rice with rabbit and snails, and *gazpachos*, here a type of game stew. Go easy on the wine, though, especially if you have been tasting – at Culebrón, they say it is strong enough to revive dead men.

13. A Morning at the Spa: Fortuna

Allow 1 hour by car from Alicante, or 45 minutes from Murcia. The spa is only open in the morning. *See map on pages 26–7.*

Murcia is something of a paradise for lovers of spa towns, with a choice of nearly half a dozen thermal baths dotted around the region. Although most have been in continual use since at least Roman times, they remain wonderfully uncommercialised and old-fashioned, with few of the luxurious trimmings or social trappings that make many spas so expensive or off-putting.

This is especially true of the three in the **Sierra de Espuña**: **Fuensanta**, tucked away an hour's drive from Lorca up a small road into the sierras and completely uncommercialised (the waters are recommended for skin treatment); **Alhama de Murcia**, in the middle of town (next to the Parque Cubana – open Monday to Saturday 9am–1pm and 4–7pm), pleasantly casual and recently restored; and **Baños de Mula**, a miniature spa-village where you can rent rooms or flats with private mineral baths inside or have a quick half hour in the baths at the top of the town (no fixed hours). For a small extra charge, it is possible to bathe in the deliciously clean, relaxing source itself.

None of these three, however, offers any treatments or massages. For this, you need to go either to Archena, sitting on the lush riverside in the Segura valley, or to Fortuna, in the dry plain north of Murcia. The baths at **Archena**, which knew glory in Roman times and the Belle Epoque, are geared up to serious pampering – marble pavements set the tone – and are unbeatable for atmosphere and setting, but are tailored to three-week courses of treatment under medical supervision rather than a lazy morning of self-indulgence (*see page 113*).

In this sense, **Fortuna** is the perfect place for spa addicts who want a quick bout of relaxation. It is sedately functional rather than elegant, but the outside world drops away once you are immersed in the deep marble baths. The waters themselves are said to be some of the best in Europe. Treatments – everything from nasal douches, needle showers and water massages to acupuncture – are so reasonably priced that you can afford to try any of them. And while you spring-clean yourself, you can enjoy the conversation of regulars who have been coming here for years.

The baths are open in the mornings only; telephone in advance (tel: 968 685 011), since there are three hotels above the spa, usually filled with people here for a series of treatments. If you want to stay in the area for the afternoon, the nearby **Saladar del Ajanque**, an arid area with salt water flooding, is interesting for its plethora of rare plants (a unique form of tamarind) and birds (eagles, etc).

This itinerary can be linked with excursions to Jumilla and Yecla (*see page 67*), via Pinoso, another wine town within the Alicante *denominación.*

14. The Sierra de Espuña

It is 1½ hours from Alicante (45 minutes from Murcia city) to the start of the Sierra de Espuña's pine forests; another hour to the furthest point, Moratalla. *See map on pages 26–7.*

Hermitage, Santa Eulalia

Unlike the Andalucian sierras, the rocky massifs of Murcia have no place in travel literature or the romantic imagination. This is a godsend since it has left them gloriously free of tourism. Yet the mountains, the tail end of the same chain, are quite as beautiful as anything further west, dropping from forested heights to crumpled chalky hills with easily accessible areas for walking. And the sierra villages, for a long time frontier towns with Muslim Granada, maintain a strong sense of their violent border history.

This semi-circular route for a two-day foray (but allow three to four for serious walking) starts at **Alhama de Murcia**'s castle ruins and thermal baths. Just beyond, at **Totana**, where flowery glazed ceramics are made, turn off for **Aledo**, stopping off at the sanctuary of **Santa Eulalia** (always open in daylight hours). A small gem with a *mudéjar* coffered ceiling, its 17th-century frescoed cartoons tell the story of a child martyr persecuted by the Romans (outside is a bar). Aledo itself was an important frontier town belonging to the Order of Santiago from the 13th to the 15th centuries, and has tremendous views and the remains of its Moorish **fortress**.

A few kilometres further along the same road is the entrance to the **Sierra de Espuña**, one of the largest nature reserves in Spain. It protects a vast area of pine forest, replanted on bare slopes in the late 19th century to stop flooding in the villages below, and flora and fauna that includes over 250 plant species, mountain cats, wild boars, native tortoises, white squirrels and rare butterflies.

Hermitage garden, Santa Eulalia

Leave the park by the eastern exit onto the road to **Pliego**, which runs through vines, almonds and olives to meet the main road to **Mula**, a historic small town sheltering under splendidly sited castle ruins (Muslim and restored in the 16th century). It keeps a clutch of churches, traditional potters and its spa baths. Then run west through Bullas to **Cehegin** (here there is a 16th-century colonnaded plaza and church undergoing emergency surgery at the top of the town). Finally, drive on to the **Caballos de Vino** inn, just outside **Caravaca de la Cruz**, for the night (*see page 111*).

A frontier town from the 11th to the 15th centuries, Caravaca is riddled with medieval mythology woven around the Knights Templar. Up in the **hermitage** built inside the **castle** you can see the church window where, it is said, angels flew in with a cross in front of the Moorish king – a bejewelled reproduction is kept in the museum (10am–1pm and 4.30–7pm; closed Monday and Sunday). The hermitage itself has a marble baroque facade, a splendid quotation out of context. Below, in the old town, wander down the pedestrianised **Calle Mayor**, catch the 16th-century **Iglesia de la Concepción** and, if you have time, drive out of town to see the Roman Temple and Bronze Age site at **La Encarnación**. The **Fuentes de el Marqués** is a beauty spot, with a quiet stretch of river, just outside town.

Try to make it to **Moratalla** in time for lunch (it has excellent country food in the bars). The seat of the Order of Santiago for centuries, it is something of a textbook fairy-tale village: backed by forested slopes, its streets wind up, as if around a snail's shell, to the 14th-century castle (the key, said to be the original, and torch for the dark tower, are kept at a nearby house). From here, the views over the fruit orchards and folded hills are splendid. The largely Gothic **church** is open only for morning and evening mass, but if you are keen to see it and the small museum with religious valuables, you can phone ahead (968 730 160).

Mountains above Moratalla

After lunch, ask for the road to the **Ermita Rogativa**, which will take you into the highest land of the province, populated only by scattered *cortijos*, or farmhouses in the Andalucian style. Pressure is mounting for all of this area to be protected, but against considerable opposition from landowners. For the time being, much wildlife remains and, if you take binoculars and are lucky, you may see some of the last herds of mountain goats.

If you have a third day, you could stay overnight in one of Moratalla's *hostales* (expect to wake early to agricultural noises) and complete the full circle. Take the road down to **Lorca**, turning off at **La Paca** to see the Argaric village at **Coy** and/or, just before you get into Lorca, to see the famous dams of **Puentes** and **Valdeinfierno**, built in the 18th century. The herby scrubland here is good walking country and between the two dams, in the middle of empty countryside, you fall upon the spa of **Fuensanta**.

15. Murcia City: Spanish Baroque

A full day exploring Murcia's unique art and architecture. *See map on page 26–7.*

Murcia can be a hard nut to crack as a tourist city. There's so much to see, yet it's easy to pass things by unless you know where to look. And in summer, the breezeless heat slows you down, beating you back off the pavements for long rests in cafés or ice cream parlours. Ideally, you need to come in spring or autumn and allow several days, so that you can wander at leisure around the shops, parks and museums, drive out of the city to see the surrounding sights and, in the mellow evenings, get under the skin of the southern street life.

If you have only one day, then it is best to concentrate your energies on the city's hoard of baroque art and architecture. It is splendid, it is unique and,

Baroque dome, La Ñora

even for northern Europeans who think they don't like baroque, it is fascinating because it captures the spirit of the place. Here, distilled in stone and marble and painted wood, are the exuberance of the fertile *huerta*, the drama of religious fervour, and the love of ornamental detail inherited from the Moorish centuries.

Start at the **Cathedral**, approaching through the **Plaza Cardinal Belluga** so that your first impression is of the superb main facade. Designed by Castilian architect and sculptor Jaime Bort, it is a perfect balance of ornament and structure, a symbolic gateway to the region, brilliantly adapted to the building and its setting. Other highlights of the Cathedral, which was looted by the French in the War of Independence, are the **Capilla de los Vélez**, its 15th-century white stone stunningly embroidered with detail inside and contrastingly severe without (it is regarded as one of the best examples of Isabelline Gothic architecture) and the cathedral **museum** (10am–1pm and 5–8pm; small admission charge).

From here, take a quick look at the crumbling **bishop's palace** and the **Iglesia de San Juan de Dios**, now revamped into a museum of religious imagery, then cross the river to the **Plaza de Camachos** (intended to be oval), where the city's bull fights were held. Both this and the **Puente Viejo**, with its curious shrine at one end, were worked on by Bort as part of the remodelling of the city centre before he was summoned to Madrid by the king. The motifs of his work – the broken arched cornice, the allegorical figures, the decorated columns – are echoed in buildings elsewhere in the city.

But the essence of Murcian baroque is the work of Francisco Salzillo (1707–83), the polychrome sculptor whose life-size painted processional figures and altarpieces adorn so many churches around the region. The realism he added to these idealised figures, capturing them in mid gesture as if with the camera shutter, gives them a heightened dramatic quality and extraordinary emotional power. In the **Museo Salzillo** devoted to his work (Pl. de San Augustín 1; Tuesday to Saturday in summer, 9.30am–1pm and 4–7pm; winter, 3–6pm; Sunday, Monday and holidays 11am–1pm) are nine massive *pasos*, processional groups that he carved between 1752 and 1778, and a collection of his nativity figures which reflect the same narrative qualities and closely observed, strongly Murcian, realism.

On the way to the museum through the old town, you pass three churches – **San Pedro, Santa Catalina, San Nicolás** – and just beyond are another trio – **San Miguel, Santa Ana** and

Casino, Murcia

Santa Clara – all with fine facades and more Salzillos. The **Iglesia de Merced** is also outstanding. As you make your way from one to another, drop off for coffee and *aperitivos* (*see Dining Experiences*).

You may also like to drive out, after lunch, to the **Monasterio de San Jeronimo** near **La Ñora**, for which Salzillo's figure in the cathedral museum was sculpted. Unadorned outside (and sometimes nicknamed the Murcian Escorial), its interior is frescoed in cobalt and ochre under a brightly painted, moulded and sculpted dome. The nuns keep the keys to the church; just ring the doorbell.

Monasterio de San Jeronimo, La Ñora

Back in town, the baroque spirit was reincarnated in Modernist form at the end of the 19th century. Among the examples scattered around the city, the **Casino**, decorated in the 1890s, is unmissable, with its wildly extravagant Arab and Pompeiian patios, and the plushest 'ladies' cloakroom' in town. (It is open all day.) The **Casa de Andrés Almansa** also has an interesting Modernist facade. They are both in the main shopping and bar area, which are a hive of activity in early evening.

Salzillo's spirit also lives on in the *belenes* or Nativity figures made by a number of craftsmen/potters (*see page 97*). Equally, the baroque spirit infuses the solemn Holy Week parades and the explosion of colour, dance and song of the springtime fiestas which follow closely on its heels.

16. Cartagena City

A morning in Cartagena's museums and old town can be extended with a trip through mining country to an unspoilt beach. *See map on pages 26–7.*

Cartagena is one of the most frustrating of all historic cities. Its prime maritime site by one of the best natural harbours of the Mediterranean speaks of its past greatness, and untold archaeological riches lie below its modern bourgeois overcoat. Yet to the casual visitor's eye the past is little in evidence and the historic monuments are forlornly empty and dilapidated.

Part of the answer lies in the city's extraordinary history. For a millennium, this was a key Mediterranean metropolis under the control of the Iberians, Phoenicians, Greeks, Carthaginians and Romans in turn. 'New Carthage is by far the most powerful of all the cities in this country,' wrote Strabo, the Roman historian, 'adorned by secure fortifications, by walls handsomely built, by harbours, by a lake and by the silver mines...'

Yet this very wealth of resources and strategic siting made the city too desirable for its own good. Stripped of its surrounding forest by the Carthaginians and Romans in order to supply fuel for the mines – Hannibal extracted 300lb of silver a day – and razed to the ground in the 7th century by the Visigothic king Sisebuto, it has never found the same glory again. To add insult to injury, periodic wartime battering and functional defensive rebuilding have, over the centuries, relentlessly eroded the traces of its past.

Modernist architecture, Cartagena

Today the city is initially unprepossessing, dominated by its naval dockyards, modern development and heavy industry – just round the corner, at **Escombreras**, is the largest oil refinery in Spain. Curiously, little is made of the rich cultural heritage under the surface (locally, this is put down to lack of funds, political deadlock and property speculation) and the main tourist 'attraction' is what is claimed to be the world's first working submarine (it almost certainly isn't), built here in 1888 by Isaac Peral. Nonetheless, if you know where to look and you have a powerful imagination, this is an intriguing place in which to spend a day exploring.

Start at the ruined **Castillo de la Concepción**, the Roman castle. The magnificent harbour that is spread below makes it immediately clear why this was once a great city. To the north lie the abandoned bullring and naval hospital, now a possible site for a *parador*. From here, you can walk down through the old town – with all its visible poverty. You will pass the ruined **Catedral Vieja**, which is thought to be one of the oldest churches in Spain and has a Roman mosaic in the crypt, and the overgrown ruins of one of two **Roman theatres**. Nearby is the **Byzantine Wall**, on show under an excellent contemporary art gallery (corner of Calle Dr Tapia and C. de la Soledad; Tuesday to Saturday 11am–1.30pm and 5.30–9pm). A similar basement excavation, this time of a Roman street under a bank, can be seen at Calle Duque 29 (open during banking hours; free).

To catch the opening hours of both archaeological museums, you then have to move quickly away from the centre of town (by taxi or a bus). The **Museo Nacional de Arqueología Maritíma** (Dique

de Navidad; Tuesday to Sunday 10am–3pm; closed Monday and holiday afternoons) houses underwater finds, many from shipwrecked boats, and a full-scale replica of a Roman galley; the **Museo Arqueológico Municipal** (C. Ramón y Cajal 45, Tuesday to Friday 10am–1pm and 4–6pm, weekends 10am–1pm), built over an important necropolis, has an excellent collection pointing up the long overlap between Iberian and Roman cultures.

Back in the central hub of the modern town, in the grid of streets laid out around the old town in 1895–7, there is some wonderful Modernist architecture which was originally paid for by industrial wealth, as in Barcelona further up the coast.

About half of this was destroyed in 1960s redevelopment, but some interesting stuff remains nonetheless: the **Casa Cervantes** and **Llagostera** in the **Calle Mayor**, the **Gran Hotel** and house at No. **27** on **Calle Jara**, and the **Palacio de Aguirre** in the **Plaza de Merced**, for example. (If you're particularly interested, the tourist of office has a full list of the buildings concerned.) These Modernist buildings, and tombs in the splendid cemetery of **Nuestra Señora de los Remedios**, are heavy with allegory and symbolism, much of it Masonic – which is said to have been handed down from the mysterious Knights Templar.

Pedestrianised and punctuated by street lights like calligraphic swirls, the heart of the old town has wonderful old-fashioned shops and lots of atmospheric bars and restaurants in which you can relax over a good lunch (such as **Columbus** at Calle Mayor 18 or **Casa Tomas**, Plaza Lopez Pinto 8).

Afterwards, the drive westward past the mines towards **Cabo de Palos** can be linked with a trip to the unspoilt beach at **Calblanque** (*see page 49*).

Cartagena casino

Entertainment

For Children and the Young at Heart

There are four **water parks** along the coast (at Cullera, Benidorm, San Juan and Torrevieja), where you can spend a day sliding and splashing about. Be warned that accidents do happen and that fatalities have been known.

Local **boat rides** go from Jávea (from June to September), Calpe (around the Peñon de Ifach, in summer only), Benidorm (to the island, all year) and most of the Mar Menor resorts (to the islands in the centre, in summer only). It is almost impossible, these days, to rent a fishing boat for a privately-tailored expedition. If you want to take a more detailed look at the local marine life without getting wet, hop aboard one of Benidorm's semi-submerged **glass-bottomed boats** (*see also ferries, page 112*).

Boats tour the **Río Safari Elche** (actually just outside Santa Pola). There are two other **safari parks**, **Verger** and **Aitana** (at Penáguila, 35km/22 miles inland from Benidorm), the biggest wildlife park in Europe. You can also see animals at Fort West, a Wild West theme park near Campello, or at **La Nucia**'s small cowboy town and zoo. Benidorm's **Mundomar Marine and Exotic Animal Park** (open 9am–6pm daily) features what is claimed to be Europe's biggest dolphinarium. See the dolphins performing morning and afternoon.

The main children's fairgrounds are **Festilandia** in Benidorm and **Festival Park** in Calpe, but they are rarely open in winter. Children might also enjoy Guadalest's two museums of miniatures, **Mundo de Max** and **1,001 Curiosities**.

If the weather conditions force you indoors in Alicante, you could pay a visit to a video game parlour or, at the other end of the scale, pleasantly fill in the time at the **Museo de Belenes** (museum of nativity scenes; Calle de la Virgen 2; Tuesday to Saturday 10.30am –2pm and 4–8pm, Sunday morning; small admission charge).

Twilight Hours

When night falls, the Costa Blanca has something on offer for everyone, and there is enough entertainment to keep you going all night if that is what you came on holiday for. In July and August, most Spaniards desert the inland towns and go on their holidays. As a result, many of the coastal resorts are somewhat lifeless out of season. In summer, a night train runs from Alicante to the resorts, running up to Denia.

Discos, Pubs and Bars

Discos and Spanish-style pubs get going around midnight, and some stay open until breakfast time, so make sure you have a good siesta. Dress is usually casual, but you might be sent home to change if you turn up in shorts.

Pubs, which are nothing like English pubs and would be better described as young bars with music, don't have entrance fees, and during the week you probably won't have to pay to get into discos either (especially if you're female). However, at weekends there may be an entrance fee. Drinks in both discos and pubs are pricey, but spirit measures are very large.

Bars are open from breakfast time until the early hours of the morning. It is usually cheaper to sit at the bar than at a table.

Alicante, Benidorm and Torrevieja are the main nightspots on the Costa Blanca itself.

Alicante/Alacant: During the summer, the action is in **San Juan** rather then Alicante itself. Wander along the seafront market (6pm–2am) and enjoy the cafés, some with live flamenco music. Pop into **Caligula**, one of San Juan's several open-air pubs. Don't be put off by the hoards of young people at the front: at the back you'll find a more relaxed atmosphere. Other pubs offer pop music, videos, swimming pools, game machines and pool tables. Away from the seafront, try **Copity** (Avda. de Condomina), one of the more classy pubs, with a mixed-age clientele. In the same road is **Va Bene**, the most popular disco, particularly with the under-25s.

During the winter or for a more quiet summer night out, start with a drink on the **Explanada**, and then go to the *barrio* **Santa Cruz**, in the old part of Alicante near the Cathedral.

This is where the bars are concentrated. Listen to jazz music in stylish **Desafinado** (just off the Rambla) or admire the imainative décor in **El Forat** (next to the Astoria cinema). Across the Rambla, **Calle San Fernando** has a host of seedy nightclubs. Big discos are **Bugatti**, Calle San Fernando 27 and **Kaos**, Calle Manero Mollá 9. **Doña Pepa**, by the town hall, is a classic old-age dance hall.

Benidorm: In summertime, every night is party night; in winter, Benidorm really comes alive only at weekends. The old pedestrian quarter is the scene of many bars and cafés. **Eros** (Calle de la Santa Faz) is a small, supposedly gay bar that is actually patronised by a mixed clientele. The main central disco is **Black Sunset**, Calle Esperanto s/n). For pubs and discos with a difference, head just out of town to the N332. You cannot fail to miss **Star Garden** (open summer only), a spaceship equipped with bars, disco, helicopter and swimming pool. Avoid **Penelope** – the biggest disco in town – and **KM** unless you enjoy 'Miss Topless' and 'Miss *Camiseta Mojada*' (wet T-shirt) competitions and other entertainment designed to appeal to the package tourist.

A little further along towards Valencia a discreet sign announces **L'Anouer** (open all year), a small, up-market bar with roguish churchy-baroque decor. In its romantic garden, candles illuminate secluded tables and pious statues. If you prefer a more modern

atmosphere, keep going until you come to **Arte** (open all year). Admire the contemporary art, enjoy the jazz/funk music and/or eat at the terrace restaurant.

Torrevieja: In the summer, open air cafés and ice cream parlours fill the streets around the port. Various pavements artists, a funfair and a market (summer, 7pm–1am) add colourful characters. In winter, Torrevieja is teeming only at weekends.

A free bus service runs between the town centre and **Chaplin Costa** (on the N332 to Alicante), a large, stylish disco for mixed age groups. You get the chance to relax in the plant-filled conservatory and the whitewashed rock garden before letting your hair down on the dance floor.

Other places: On the coast, **Altea's** old quarter (behind the beach) is full of bars and restaurants. In both **Calpe** and **Denia**, the action takes place along the beach – winter weekends and summer only. The busiest area in **Cartagena** is the **Cuesta de la Baronesa** (near the Cathedral), where there are many pubs and cafés; other areas include the **Calle Cuatro Santos** and **Calle Bodegones**. In **Santa Pola**, the bars in the town centre (near the port) cater mainly for the younger generation. Among the good discos are **Camelot**, **El Cano** and **Bolero**.

Elche's own entertainment is situated right in the heart of the town, while **Orihuela**'s is practically non-existent. Murcia and Alcoi are generally pretty dead in July and August, but buck up considerably in spring and autumn. **La Buggate** is the zone to head for in **Murcia**, while bars in **Alcoi** are concentrated in the **Santa Rosa** district and around the **Pl. España**.

Shows

For glorious tackiness, you can't beat the expensive extravaganza at the mock castle, **Castillo Fortaleza de Alfaz**, 7kms (4 miles) from Benidorm just off the N332 to Altea. A mediocre medieval banquet features jousting and duelling. Then the chamber of horrors leads up to the futuristic disco with its multiple video screens and lasers. **Benidorm Palace**, near **Aqualandia** on the eastern outskirts of town, is reminiscent of a Blackpool show hall. Catering with a vengeance for the international crowd, it offers 'Spanish style' cabaret and the occasional one-off concert (Julio Iglesias started his career at the Benidorm Palace).

Casinos

You won't de admitted without showing your passport (minimum age 18). Dress is casually smart; they are used to tourists so they do not have a strict dress code.

Benidorm: **Casino Costa Blanca**, 5kms (3 miles) from Benidorm on the N332 towards Villajoyosa, open all year 9pm–4am; entrance fee; drinks at pub prices. Games include blackjack, *chemin de fer* and roulette. Cash dispenser in the foyer for credit cards and Eurocheques!

Murcia: There is a luxury casino in Calle Apóstoles 34.

For Culture Vultures

Theatre and concerts: There are three theatres in **Alcoi**, two of which also show films. All are in or near the **Pl. de España. Elche** and **Murcia** each have one theatre, of which the most important and lively is the **Teatro Romea** in Murcia. Many towns have a **Casa de Cultura**, where concerts and other cultural events takes place. The local savings banks also have auditoriums that host a variety of events, often free.

Most musical performances are grouped in seasons or festivals; the most important of these are the **International Contemporary Music Festival** in Alicante (mid-September), the **International Jazz Festival** in Murcia (the week after Easter) and regional music festivals. In the summer, performances are staged in open air amphitheatres in Alcoi, Benidorm and Elche. In Alicante, the **Castillo de Santa Bárbara** and the **Pl. de Toros** are both used as venues for various concerts and galas.

Cinemas

There are cinemas in the large towns, as well as summer open-air and drive-in cinemas in the coastal resorts. The **Astoria**, in the *barrio* **Sant Cruz** in **Alicante**, occasionally shows English-language films in the original. Many cinemas offer cheap tickets on one particular night of the week.

Bullfighting

Spaniards discuss endlessly whether this is a sport, a stylised art form or a barbarian form of torture. You will have to decide whether the sight of a bull being gradually weakened for the kill is for you.

The standard of bullfighting in the area is generally high, especially in **Alicante** (the best time is the end of June) and **Ondara** (*see page 31*). There are other bullrings in **Benidorm, Cartagena, Murcia** (best in the first week of September) and **Torrevieja**, as well as occasional temporary rings in other tourist centres for displays by junior *toreros*.

Ticket prices vary considerably between and within each bullring, depending on the quality of the *toreros* and on where you sit. It is worth paying the extra to sit in the shade during the summer and also to hire a cushion, because the spectacle lasts about 2½ hours or more. Be warned that an agency will charge up to 20 percent more than the standard price, and a hotel will charge up to 40 percent more.

Dining Ex

Local Cooking

The cooking of eastern Spain is a remarkably straightforward mirror of its tripartite geography: the sea and the mountains – the classic *montaña y mar* of so much Spanish coastal cuisine – and, most important of all in the regions of Valencia and Murcia, the fertile plains transformed into a massive market garden by Moorish irrigation. As you drive south, it is this coastal strip, thoroughly tamed and carefully tended, which sticks in the memory.

Equally, it is the produce of the plains – oranges and lemons, rice, almonds, orchard fruit and a huge range of vegetables – which differentiates the local cooking from that elsewhere on the Mediterranean coast. Lighter in touch than Catalan cuisine and peppered with clear Moorish influences, it has a temperate abundance distinct from the frying, stews and salads of the sun-baked south.

Rice is the great common denominator. *Paella*, which started out here in Valencia as poor country food made with rabbit and snails, is the most famous local dish, but it is only one of the vast extended family of *arroces*, or rices, and often the worst choice in restaurants, since it tends to be tailored to tourist expectations. Don't be put off by humbler combinations – they can be the most delicious. From the coast come *arroz abanda* and *caldero*, both made with stock from the small rock

Fisherman's favourite, 'arroz abanda'

eriences

fish that fishermen could not sell in the old days; on the plains, vegetables and pork products flavour various *paella huertanos* and *arroz con costra*; in the mountains, *arroces serranos* are typically flavoured with snails, herbs from the sierras and local game such as rabbit.

In other dishes, too, the tripartite geographical division holds true. Fish dishes are widely available inland, but usually at their best in ports. Denia's monster prawns and *arroz abanda*, Santa Pola's *gazpacho de mero*, a fish stew served on flatbread, Cabo de Palo's salt-baked fish and grey mullets' roe (*huevos de mújol*) – a Mediterranean caviar – all gain from on-the-spot freshness and local sleight of hand. Shellfish is generally good if it's local, but falling catches have sent prices sky-high. Guardamar's *langostinos*, for example, can cost up to £50 a kilo. These days genuine *salazones* or salted fish products such as *mojama* (salted tuna), products of a tradition that goes back to Phoenician times, have also become elevated to luxuries, like the prize local hams.

Inland, especially in the sierras, traditional cooking is often more Castilian than Mediterranean. Humble dishes such as the *migas* based on breadcrumbs, *gazpachos*, tasty shepherds' game-and-poultry stews served on top of a flatbread (which originally served as the plate as well) and *trigo picado*, a cracked wheat stew, have appeared on restaurant menus in the last few years and are well worth trying.

In the Alicante mountains, the food becomes more warming:

Quenching thirst, local style

soups, stews (*ollas*) and other dishes based on dried beans, *bacalao* (salt-cod) or cured meats, cooked with saffron and the herbs of the sierras. The most famous of these are *olleta* and *giraboix*, stews which are at their best in winter in the *ventas* (old coaching inns) and *pericana*, griddled salt-cod, flaked then seasoned with dried peppers, garlic and olive oil. The four main vineyard areas – Monóvar and Gorgos valley in Alicante, Jumilla and Yecla in Murcia – are especially strong on these robust country dishes.

Down on the fertile plains the most varied cooking, sensual and highly coloured, is that of the Murcia *huerta*. Characteristic seasonings here are green garlic and *pimentón* – sweet paprika ground down from local *noria* peppers – and the most original dishes are those using the huge range of locally grown fruit and vegetables. Further north, in Alicante, *coques*, first cousins to Italian pizzas, use the same Mediterranean vegetables on crispy, thin pastry crusts. There are less obvious products typical of the *huertas* too: sweet pork and poultry fattened up on fruit and corn, which go into various sausages and *relleno* (rissoles), and delicious honey from the Alicante *huerta*.

Freshly baked in Benissa

As rice is to savoury dishes, so oranges, lemons and almonds are to sweet things. The oranges and lemons appear in huge mounds on road side stalls (only buy in season), in fruit tarts and as glacé fruit, while the almonds are used in countless different cakes, biscuits, puddings, liqueurs and sweets. The most remarkable among these is *turrón*, a kind of nougat, which is wolfed down by the Spanish in huge quantities at Christmas.

Cooling summer drinks and ices are another local forte, said to be inherited from the Moors. Whether you're buying an ice cream, *granizada* (icy slush made from lemon, orange or coffee) or *horchata* (an addictive chalky, semi-frozen nut-milk made from ground *chufas*, plus sugar and water), there is an enormous difference between more expensive versions made from natural products and sickly, cheap ones bought in from big factories, so try and look for a sign saying *propria fabricación* or *artesanal*. For the local wines, or *vinos de país*, which can be found in most restaurants, see the relevant itineraries and options.

Eating Out

In general, eating out is cheap, varied and cosmopolitan near the coast, and it is easy to find standard fast food and a selection of ethnic restaurants in the main resorts. The listing in this guide therefore concentrates on good local cooking, which is trickier to locate for the outsider.

Restaurants: These are listed on the next page by place name, in alphabetical order, with an indication of area when outside major towns and resorts. This is a personal and necessarily limited selection; if you want to get down to some really serious eating, it is best to invest in the Campsa guide.

Complaints: As in hotels, a complaints book is available for use by dissatisfied customers. Check that mineral water is the real thing (beware if the bottle isn't opened at the table) or you may be drinking expensive tap water.

Opening Times: Holidays are erratic; many restaurants away from major tourist zones close on Sunday evenings (or all day in city centres) and for one to two months during the summer – it is therefore advisable to phone in advance to check a place is open. Standard kitchen hours are 1pm–4pm and 7.30pm to midnight (occasionally until 11pm). Most Spaniards do not eat lunch until 2pm and then wait until 10pm for dinner, but restaurants in tourist areas are used to people eating earlier than this and have adjusted their times accordingly.

Payment: Do not rely on paying by credit card outside smart city centre restaurants; cards accepted, if at all, vary enormously. Prices may or may not include IVA (VAT), but it is usual to tip a small percentage in addition.

Restaurant Grading: Restaurants are graded in four classes, plus de Luxe, but the grading often refers to the decor, the number of dishes on the menu and the price of the set tourist menu, rather than the quality of the food and service.

Cooperative bar, Parcent

Snacks: If you want a light meal, many bars and *cervecerias* serve a selection of *tapas*, small dishes of tasty snacks which are eaten alongside a drink. They come in three sizes: *pinchos* (a mouthful, sometimes offered free), *tapas* (around a saucerful), and *raciones* (a small plateful). You pay at the end rather than as you go along.

Vegetarianism: While self-catering for vegetarians is a pleasure here because the range and quality of fruit and vegetables are so good (but bring more obscure health-food products with you), Spanish restaurants are not generally geared up for the non-meat eater. However, you can nearly always get a plain *tortilla* and salad, or a selection of vegetable *tapas*. Two useful eating places are a vegan restaurant in C. Turrones, Murcia, and a vegetarian restaurant next to Santa Ana church, Alicante.

Recommended Restaurants

Agres (northern Alicante)

PENSION MARIOLA, Calle San Antonio 4, tel: 96 551 0017. Large country dining room. Local dishes: *batjoques fasides* (peppers stuffed with rice), rabbit with garlic, *pericana.* Closed mid-September to October.

Alcantarilla (central Murcia)

MESON DE LA HUERTA, Avda. del Príncipe s/n, tel: 968 802 390. Echoing the traditional inn, this restaurant is next door to the Museo de la Huerta with excellent *tapas* and full meals based on the surrounding *huerta*'s vegetable produce. Recommended puddings include *papajarotes,* double-sided pancakes fried on lemon leaves, accompanied by a sweet liqueur sauce.

Alicante/Alacant (city)

DARSENA, Muelle de Levante 6, tel: 96 520 7399. Closed Sunday evenings, Mondays in summer. Unbeatable for rice dishes – over 20 on the menu – and also good for fish. More relaxed at dinner than lunch.

LA GOLETA, Explanada de España 8, tel: 96 521 4392. Reasonably priced seafood restaurant.

NOU MANOULIN, C. Villegas 3, tel: 96 520 0368. Good daily regional dishes and *tapas* taken up-market, backed up by one of the best cellars on the Mediterranean. Good value.

Castalla (Southern Alicante)

MESON EL VISCAYO, Camino La Bola s/n, tel: 96 556 0196. Known for its good herby mountain *gazpachos* and homemade breads. Farmhouse atmosphere.

Bañeres (Banyeres)

Venta El Borrego, Ctra Villena-Ontenienle km18. Traditional inn renowned for its herby mountain *gazpachos* and game stews.

Benidorm

L'Esclau, Bon Retiro. Excellent city centre fish restaurant with largely local clientele. Photos of old Benidorm on the walls set the atmosphere. Closed Sunday and Monday.

La Rana, Costera del Barco 6, Casa Antig (or smaller branch at La Raneta, C. Martinez Oriola 25). The Arroyos owned the first eating house before tourism hit. Now they concentrate on *tapas*, which you can snack on or build into a meal. Quality produce, very central.

El Molino, Ctra Valencia km123, tel: 96 585 7181, closed Monday and from 1 October to 1 November. El Molino is done up like an old inn, with a forest of wine bottles hanging from the ceiling and reliable international food. Also offers a summer terrace.

Cabo de Palos (central Murcia)

La Tana, Paseo de la Barra 33, tel: 968 563 003, closed Monday except in summer. Cabo is the place to eat *caldero*, the Mar Menor's answer to *paella*, and sea bass (or, more traditionally, mullet) in salt.

Caravaca de la Cruz (central Murcia)

Caballos del Vino, Ctra de Murcia 71, tel: 968 702 219. One of the Sierra de Espuña's few restaurants with lots of interesting, local dishes, e.g *olla caravaquena*, *tartera de pollo*, *migas caravaquenas*. Kitchen open all day. Accommodation is available above the restaurant.

Cocentaina (northern Alicante)

Venta del Pilar, Ctra Valencia s/n, Termino de Cocentaina, tel: 96 559 2325. Closed Easter, August, and Sundays. Renowned 18th-century coaching inn. Classics are *olleta*, roast lamb, orange tart and home-made *aguardientes* (lethal *eaux-de-vie*). Also has an international menu.

Denia

El Pegoli, Baret de Les Rotes, tel: 96 578 1035. Memorable family restaurant worth a special expedition. The formula is a set menu of giant prawns from the bay, *arroz abanda* and fresh fruit, or fish and shellfish paid for by weight. If it's full, try El Trampoli or Mesón Troya.

Elche/Elx

Bar-Meson Arlequin, Pl. de Santa Maria/Congresu, s/n. Noisy tavern opposite the cathedral with *arroz con costra*, and other local dishes. Very good value.

Els Capellans, Porta de la Morera 14, tel: 96 545 8040. One of three restaurants within the Hort del Cura hotel. Gracious and very smart, surrounded by the famous palm trees. Its menu is an imaginative hybrid of international and local cuisine, as in dishes such as palm-heart salad and sweet date omelette. Els Capellas is one of the more expensive restaurants in this listing.

El Palmar (southern Valencia)

Raco de L'Olla, C. Valencia-El Palmar km 9, tel: 96 162 0172 Lunch only, closed Monday from September–June; closed on Sunday in July–August; closed for ten days in January, open evenings in winter on Friday and Saturday. The place to eat the dishes of the Albufera, *all-i-pebre* and *paella*. In El Palmar itself there are cheaper, but perfectly good restaurants.

Gata de Gorgos (northern Alicante)

Corral Del Pato, Partida Trossets. Ctra Jalón km 1, tel: 96 575 6834. A converted farmhouse run as family restaurant, which offers excellent local cooking.

Jalón/Xaló (northern Alicante)

Terrases de la Torre, Ctra Gata de Gorgos-Xaló, tel: 96 573 3204. Highly recommended locally for country Alicantino cooking: pickles, rice dishes, game, sausages, etc. Winter (October–April) open Friday–Sunday only.

Játiva/Xàtiva (Valencia)

Fonda Casa Floro, Pl. del Mercat 46, tel: 96 227 3020. Good country food, packed on market days. *Arroz al horno* and *gazpachos*. Closed August.

Jumilla (north Murcia)

Casa Sebastian, Mercado de Abastos, Avda. de Levante 6, tel: 96 780 194. Closed first two weeks in August. Highly recommended market restaurant serving breakfast and lunch until 4.15pm. Solidly provincial cooking with big rounded flavours to match local wines (18,000 bottles in the cellar).

Murcia (city)

El Corral de Jose Luis, Pl. Santo Domingo 14–15, Murcia, tel: 968 214 597. Busy central restaurant with a wide range of excellent local *tapas* at the bar or full-scale sit-down meals. Very reasonable prices. An alternative is **El Churra**, Avda Maqués de los Vélez 12, tel: 283 400.

El Rincon de Pepe, Apóstoles 34, tel: 96 212 239. The first restaurant to bring Murcian cooking to national attention. Hard to fault either on the daily menu or the *à la carte*. Take guidance on Murcian specialities.

Pinoso (southern Alicante)

Alfonso, Pl. España 4, tel: 96 547 7820. Country restaurant known for its *serrano*, with local white snails and roast garlic. Mid-price.

Santa Pola

Meson del Puerto, C. Astilleros 3, tel: 96 541 1289. Cheaper and more local than most of the fish restaurants, with *gazpacho de mero* – a fish stew served on flatbread – and *caldero*. Closed mid-December to mid-January.

La Naveta, C. Poeta Miguel Hernandez 15, tel: 96 541 6765. In the centre of town, near the fortress/museum

Sax (central Alicante)

Meson el Almendros, Cruce las Cuatros Rosas 99, tel: 96 547 5032. Good charcoal grilled food (for example, bream, sea bass, lamb) and other local dishes. Handy for the Madrid–Alicante motorway. Closed two weeks in August.

Tàrberna (northern Alicante)

Casa Pinet, Plaza Mayor, tel: 96 588 1362. Country cooking in light-hearted political (revolutionary) atmosphere. Excellent *olla*.

Totana (central Murcia)

Bar-Restaurante La Santa, Santuario La Santa, tel: 968 426 377. All meals to order. Informal short-menu country restaurant by the sanctuary; busy Sunday lunch.

Villajoyosa/La Vila Joiosa

El Pachel, Partida de la Ermita 28, tel: 96 589 0003. Very fresh seafood and fish dishes – alternatively try the inexpensive restaurants down by the fishing quarter.

Shopping

Spain is no longer the budget holiday destination it once was, so do not expect to find many dirt-cheap bargains, even if you buy locally-made items such as clothes and shoes. However, you do get what you pay for: leather goods, in particular, are very well made.

The coast itself is not abundantly rich in local crafts, and those that exist are being gradually squeezed out by mass production. Nevertheless, there is an enticing array of local food and wine. Inland areas, especially Murcia, have kept their crafts, often Moorish-influenced, and they provide the most interesting souvenirs. In large towns, small local shops are having to compete with department stores (**El Corte Inglés**), supermarkets and hypermarkets (**Continente, Pryca, Hiper Todo, Mamut**).

Most shops are open Monday to Friday 10am–1.30pm and 5–8pm, and on Saturday 10am–1.30pm. Some bakeries and newsagents also open for a few hours on Sunday mornings. Department stores, hypermarkets and large supermarkets stay open during the siesta, so this is a good time to shop if you want to avoid the crowds. You will need to be self-assertive but polite when shopping (especially

in markets); queues are uncommon, and it is up to the shopper to demand attention. In some small shops, on the other hand, browsing can become embarrassing because of well-meaning but over-attentive shop assistants.

Markets

All neighbourhoods in Spain have municipal foodmarkets (*mercados*), which are often the cheapest places to buy fresh produce. General street markets (*mercadillos*) are best for buying things like rope-soled sandals (*alpargatas*), relatively cheap clothing, household goods such as *paella* pans, etc. It is worth trying your hand at bartering – you may be surprised by your success.

It is best to arrive at markets as early as possible in the day: most are well underway by 8.30am; by 10am you may find them uncomfortably busy. They stay open until 1.30 or 2pm, but in food markets the best produce is often gone by then. A selection of markets is listed below.

Alicante/Alacant

Thursday and Saturday, 8.30am–1.30pm. Campoamor (near Pl. de Toros). Wide range of goods from fruit and vegetables to clothes.
Daily, particularly evenings. Esplanada. Jewellery, leather goods, cheap watches, etc.

Altea

Tuesday, 8am–1.30pm. By the port. Very tourist-orientated; cheap jeans, pearls from Mallorca, etc. You need to look hard for local goods.

Dénia

Monday, 8am–2pm. By the railway station. Almonds, raisins, fig cake, etc.

Játiva/Xàtiva

Tuesday and Thursday mornings. Pl. del Mercat. Good mixture of small country stalls, as you would expect in an inland, agricultural, market town.

Murcia

Daily. Pl. de las Flores. Flower market.

Santa Pola

Daily 5-6pm. At the port. Auction of fresh fish direct from the boats. Stalls outside also sell fish in small quantities.

Local Crafts

If you are keen to buy local crafts, try to get hold of the government-backed *Guías de artesanía* for Alicante and Murcia, which give complete listings. The following towns are known for particular local industries, and are therefore good places to buy the relevant products. **Abarán**: *esparto* grass mats; **Agost**: pottery; **Alcoi**: sugar-coated almonds; **Crevillente**: glassware, rugs and carpets, wickerwork and *esparto* grass; **Denia**: raisins; **Elche**: shoes; **Elda**: shoes and lace; **Gata de Gorgos**: cane and basket work; **Guadalest**: leather goods, shawls and lace work; **Ibi**: toys; **Jijona**: *turrón*; **Murcia city**: carved figurines; **Valencia city**: fans; **Villajoyosa**: chocolate. **Lorca** is a main craft centre: each year it organises a large, Easter Week Fair.

Agost

POTTERY: **Museo d'Alfarería**, C. Teulería 11, tel: 96 569 1199. Closed Monday. Good range, including pots from Biar. At the Tibi entrance to town are **Pedro Molla** (traditional functional items) and **Emili Boix** (decorative, modern ceramics). All sell traditional white earthenware water bottles (*botijos*) fired in old Arab kilns.

Alicante/Alacant

CERAMICS: **V. Pascual**, Avda. Alfonso Sabio 15, tel: 96 514 0139. Unglazed, glazed and painted pottery in traditional Alicante and Valencia styles.

ESPADRILLES: **Alpargatería Ortega**, C. General Primo de Rivera 12, tel: 96 521 4853. All kinds of rope-soled sandals, including traditional *alpargatas alicantinas* (white with black ribbons) and the harder-wearing leather country ones.

TURRON: **Turrones Teclo**, C. Mayor 23, tel: 96 520 1115. Old-fashioned outlet of a Jijona factory, selling all kinds of *turrón*, caramelised almonds and other confectionery.

Elche/Elx

SHOES: **Artesana del Calzado**, Carr. Murcia–Alicante, tel: 96 667 5441. Lets you see the shoes being made. Also numerous factory outlets on the N340.

Jalón/Xalón

HONEY: **L'Abella**, Avda. Juan Carlos I 21. All kinds of honey from various parts of Spain. Bee-keeping-owner also makes and sells almond-blossom honey, furniture wax and candles.
WINE: **Bodega Cooperativa Virgen Pobre**, Carr. Xalón–Alacalí s/n, tel: 96 648 0034. Look out for the 1981 and 1987 vintages. Good reds, rosés and sweet *mistela.*

Jijona

TURRON: **Museo de Turrón El Lobo**, C. Alcoi 62, tel: 96 561 0225. This shop, attached to the *turrón* (nougat) factory, sells a huge range.

Jumilla

WINE: **Bodegas San Isidro**, Carr. de Murcia s/n (on road to Yecla at La Alquería), tel: 968 780 700. Best known for red wines. Also has a shop in the town centre selling everything from vintage wines to kitschy gifts.

Lorca

CRAFTS: **Centro Regional de Artesanía**, C. Lope Gisbert s/n, tel: 968 463 912. Permanent exhibition hall and two for temporary exhibitions, as well as archives of local crafts.
EMBROIDERY: **Joaquín Castellar**, C. Corredera 35, tel: 968 466 646. Workshop based on local tradition of lace and embroidery.
POTTERY: **El Lareo**, Carretera Murcia 23, tel: 968 468 183.

Murcia

CARVED FIGURINES (BELENES): **Manuel Nicolás Almansa**, C. Belenes 12, Santiago el Mayor, tel: 968 255 858; **Artesanía Hnos. Griñán**, Calle de la Iglesia, Puente Tocinos, tel: 968 301 640. In the 18th-century Francisco Salzillo style. Two of a dozen or so *belén*-makers still working in the studio.
CRAFTS: **Centro Regional de Artesanía**, C. Francisco Rabal, tel: 968 284 585. Excellent cooperative for local crafts at workshop prices.

Villajoyosa/La Vila Joiosa

CHOCOLATE: **Chocolatería Buana**, Avda. País Valencia 10, tel: 96 589 1006. Buy solid chocolate to take away, or stay for hot chocolate and *churros*. Also **Chocolatería Valor** in the same street.

SPORTS

The Costa Blanca's great outdoors seduces the most sedentary holidaymaker into action. Make the most of the Mediterranean, the mountains and the marvellous weather.

On and In the Water

The warm calm Mediterranean is a paradise for water sports enthusiasts. The Mar Menor, immediately south of the present-day Costa Blanca, is particularly noteworthy. If you don't have your own equipment, hire it either on the beach or from one of the several nautical clubs, where you can probably sign up for lessons too.

Wind surfers and small **sailing** dinghies may be hired on many beaches, but La Manga is best for the serious wind-surfer or sailor. Calpe is the only place for **parasailing**. If the wind drops, hire a **speedboat** at Benidorm or **jet skis** at Denia or Xàbia (Jávea) and let an engine do the work.

Water-skiing, available at many resorts, is an expensive sport to try. Check beforehand the length of the run, the permitted number of falls, and possible discounts for multiple runs. A cheaper alternative is **cable skiing** off the Playa de Levante in Benidorm.

You could also power yourself under your own steam in a **pedal boat**, or try canoeing inland at Beniarrés dam.

The Amadorio dam (near Villajoyosa) and Guadalest dam are good places for fresh water **fishing**. You will need to obtain a licence from the relevant government department, the

Consellería d'Agricultura i Pesca, C. Professor Manel Sala 2, Alicante (tel: 96 593 4000). Ask for details in a tourist information office or fishing tackle shop. Local fish include *barbel* (carp), bass and rainbow trout.

You are unlikely to catch anything big from the sea without the expert advice of a local fisherman, but the possible rewards for your efforts include grey mullet, sea bream, bass, grouper, mackerel, dorada, tuna and swordfish.

Snorkelling and **sub-aqua** are excellent in certain areas that have protected the submarine flora and fauna. Popular haunts include the Playa de Barraca (southeast of Jávea), the Peñón de Ifach (Calpe), Playa de Torres (just east of Villajoyosa), Cabo de las Huertas (San Juan), the Cabo de Palos (La Manga) and the islands of Benidorm and Tabarca.

For **sub-aqua**, a diving centre can usually provide a diving permit (also available from the *Consellería d'Agricultura* as above), equipment, a boat, tuition and tips about the local area.

Snorkellers who swim away from the shore must tow a marker buoy, for safety reasons. Watch out for sea urchins, wear flippers or plastic shoes when snorkelling or swimming near cliffs and rocks, and be careful where you put you hands.

You will not, of course, have such problems in a swimming pool. You may be able to take a dip at your hotel or campsite. If not, inland towns such as Elche and Murcia have a public outdoor pool, and most large towns have an indoor one.

On Land

Motorised thrills and spills are more enjoyable off the road than on: take out your aggressions by **go-karting**, available at many places along the coast. For fun on smaller wheels, go **roller-skating** (rinks at Jávea, Calpe, Benidorm and Alicante).

If you like to keep your feet firmly on the ground, there are various mountain ranges that offer **walking/mountaineering** to heights of 1,500m (4,875ft). Major areas include the Sierra de Espuña to the south, and the sierras within the triangle formed by Alcoi, Denia and Benidorm. Calpe boasts the Peñón de Ifach (333m or 1,090 ft), the most famous climbing face, but there are also many others. Experienced riders can go **horseback riding** in the mountains. Novices may have to make do with lessons in the paddock. For details of all these, ask in tourist offices.

Cycletourism has also taken off here in recent years. Tourist information offices can supply information on hiring bikes and routes graded by difficulty.

Enjoy the scenery from one of the area's many **golf** courses. All are open to visitors on payment of green fees. Caddies are not usually available, but most clubs hire out equipment. The course at El Saler, near Albufera south of Valencia is particularly famous. There are also courses at Xàbia (Jávea), Calpe, Altea, Torrevieja and La Manga, beside the Mar Menor.

Still outdoors, some hotels have **tennis** courts, and non-residents can often play on them for a fee. At Villajoyosa there is a three-star hotel/apartment complex (Eurotennis, tel: 96 589 1250) specialising in tennis holidays. Many towns have tennis clubs that are open to non-members.

Beaches

This is a brief, selective guide to help choose a beach (*playa* or *platja*), either for a quick visit in combination with one of the itineraries or for a long, lazy day's sunbathing and swimming. It also includes a few of the Costa Cálida beaches, redefined apart from the Costa Blanca in the late 1970s, which are within close reach of inland areas explored by the itineraries.

Broadly speaking, the Costa Blanca falls into two halves: the northern bays and coves running down from Denia to Alicante, which are divided by rocky headlands and backed by mountains, and the flat shoreline stretching south from Alicante to the regional border with Murcia and the Mar Menor. The northern half is the more heavily developed – including the high-rise international beach resorts of Calpe, Benidorm and Alicante – but the lush vegetation hides a multitude of sins where there is only low-level villa development.

There are some surprisingly good beaches here: the rocky inlets of **Les Rotes**, south of Denia; the **Mar Azul** opposite **Portitxol**, the **Playa de Granadellas** and **Cala de los Tiestos** on the Cabo de la Nao; the coves north of Calpe, such as **Fustera** and **Pinets**, pebbly **L'Albir**, north of Benidorm, and the bays south of Villajoyosa, such as **Cala del Xarco**. Many of these can be reached by rail as well as road.

In Alicante itself, **Postiguet**, the city centre beach, has a more local feel than **San Juan** or **La Albufereta**, while the **Cabo de la Huerta**, badly sign-posted (perhaps deliberately, and why not?), manages to hold off development and is good for snorkelling off the rocks.

South of Alicante, beaches are emptier and the development less continuous, but the high-rise resorts and villa estates stand out more brutally against oriental flatness. **Los Arenales** – within close range of Elche

Isla de Portixol

– has awful apartment blocks, but is a good stretch of gently sloping sand for children. **Tabarca**, Santa Pola's island, is inundated in summer because of the breeziness of its small beach, but its coves have some of the most interesting submarine life of the whole coast.

Of the other beaches between here and the Mar Menor, **Guardamar** has a good patch by the fishermen's huts next to the river mouth, and **Dehesa de Campoamor** (a 20-minutes drive from Orihuela) has kept some unspoilt coves below rocky cliffs before you run into the main development as you drive south.

San Pedro del Pinatar, the first main Murcian resort, marks a shift to the warm, calm shallows, greyish sand and largely Spanish family tourism of the inland Mar Menor resorts. They are quietest between Los Alcázares and Los Nietos, where you can look over to the long sandy spit of **La Manga**, packed out (and deluged by traffic) in summer. But the best beaches are round the corner. Known collectively as **Calblanque**, they have glassy-clear water, skin-diving and a rare wide horizon of undeveloped coast protected as *parque natural*.

Finally, south of Cartagena, **San Ginés** is an unspoilt narrow crescent of sand with old-fashioned beach houses and lots of families from the city at weekends.

Nude Sunbathing

It is quite usual for women to sunbathe topless on the principal beaches of the Costa Blanca and Costa Calida, and it is not likely to offend local people. Nude sunbathing is permittedm on the following beaches: **Ambolo** (Cabo de la Nao), **Los Judios** (Cabo de las Huertas), **El Saladar** (south of Alicante city), **El Carabassi** (Elche district), **Los Tusales San Juan** (Guardamar), **Portus** (just north of Cartagena).

Blue Flags

Costa Blanca and Costa Calida beaches have a clean record. Many of them have been awarded the EU 'Blue Flag' standards for cleanliness, safety and amenities – more than any other coast. Busy beaches have lifeguards, Red Cross posts and sometimes rescue boats as well.

The lifeguards fly a green flag when the water is safe, a yellow flag when swimmers should be careful and a red one if sea conditions are dangerous.

Calendar of Special Events

Fiestas – or *festas* in *Valenciano* – are a way of life in Spain, fusing solemn historic traditions, usually linked to the religious and agricultural year, with regional customs and the exhausting native stamina for partying. Many traditional fiestas were banned under Franco (*carnaval* in most places), but have been revived since his death.

There are now so many fiestas, both small and large, that it is impossible to list them all. This brief calendar, organised around the type of fiesta, has a bias towards traditional popular culture and fiestas in which it is easiest for outsiders to join. Dates and places are given whenever possible, but many are general and/or move around with the religious calendar. Ask for details at tourist offices or town halls when you arrive.

January 5–6

Los Reyes Magos: On the eve of Epiphany, parades in towns all over Spain celebrate the arrival of the Three Kings by various modes of transport: for example, camel, boat (Alicante city and Cartagena), horse, tractor, helicopter, etc. In Aledo and Cañada (near Villena), there are *autos*, or religious plays, on 6 January.

'Hogueras' festivals, Alicante (June)

January 17–19

San Antón: Some of the most typical countryside celebrations, with the blessing of animals, parades of carts and horses and cooking competitions. In Alicante town, there is a craft fair.

Mid-February–beginning of Lent

Carnaval: Iberian carnival, originally a great pre-Lenten meat-eating feast, has come back in an uproariously secular way in the last 20 years, with fancy-dress – a lot of it transsexual – dancing through the night, big street parades and no stinting on the drink.

Mid-March

Fallas (Valencia city): One of Spain's biggest fiestas, which originated in the 15th century with furniture makers' and carpenters' bonfires on the day of their patron saint, St Joseph. Worth a special trip to see the extraordinary bonfire effigies, which cost millions of pesetas to build and are left on display around the streets. On the 19th, they are all burned to the ground. Beware: for hotels and parking, the city is bursting at the seams.

Holy Week

Semana Santa: The processions all over Spain between Palm Sunday and Good Friday are interesting for their brotherhoods, which originated in various ways over the centuries (among the aristocracy, crafts guilds, neighbourhood groups or churches), and for their ritual and fervour. Those of Murcia city – and region – are specially rated for their *pasos*, or processional images, by 18th-century sculptor Salzillo, and Lorca's for their baroque pageantry.

Particularly noteworthy, with the days of the most important processions indicated where relevant are: Callosa de Segura (Wednesday and passion play on Good Friday); Cartagena (Wednesday, Friday and Sunday); Crevillente; Elche (Palm Sunday procession in the town where all the Easter palms come from); Jumilla (Tuesday and Sunday); Lorca (procession famed for the rivalry of the two brotherhoods, Azul and Blanco, on Good Friday); Mula and Moratalla (*tamborada* drumming Wednesday, Thursday, Friday); Murcia city (Los Coloraos, Wednesday; Silencio, Thursday; Los Salzillos, Friday); Orihuela. On Easter Monday in Alicante, people troop out into the country with Easter breads, called *monas*, for picnics.

Thursday after Holy Week

La Peregrina de la Santa Faz (Alicante city, Thursday after Holy Week): Over 100,000 people make a 5km/3 mile pilgrimage out from the city for mass and picnic at the Monastery of Santa Faz, drinking sweet *Fondillón* wine to keep up their energy.

April

Fiestas de Perimavera (Murcia city and surrounding villages): Spring festivals. A cross between a huge horticultural show and folklore festival, the most traditional elements being the *Bando de la Huerta* – dancing, singing and satirical flower-laden floats – and the *Entierro de la Sardina*, literally 'Burial of the Sardine', marking the end of Lent.

Pentecost Sunday

Festa del Xop (Planes): This is the oldest fiesta of Alicante province, held to guarantee fertility; a poplar tree is uprooted and planted in the main plaza and then scaled by the village's bachelors.

April–September

Moros y Cristianos (Alcoi, April 22-24; Caravaca, early May; Jijona, late August; Lorca, September; Orihuela, late July; Villajoyosa, end of July; Villena, early September): typically Alicatino, going back to the 17th century at least, the fiestas commemorate the Christian reconquest with parades of elaborately costumed Moors and Christians (the groups usually grew out of the craft guilds), parleys between the two sides and a mock battle – leading to a Christian victory of course. Lots of bangers, gunpowder and fireworks along the way. Alcoi's, on St George's day, are the best known for their sumptuous costumes and atmosphere, but others take place throughout the year (in 45 places in Alicante province alone) on various saints' days. Variations include the Moors' arrival by boat at Villajoyosa and, at Caravaca de la Cruz, the *Caballos de Vino*, a 17th-century horse race based on the Knights Templar once breaking the Moorish siege to fetch drinking water, but coming back with wine instead.

Mid-May

San Pascual (Orito, near Novelda): One of the smallest images of the Virgin in Spain is taken out of the Franciscan monastery for a pilgrimage up to the cave where San Pascual meditated. People come from all over the region for the value of the water, said to cure skin ailments.

May or June

Corpus Christi: Formal religious processions and, sometimes, jollification in many towns and villages.

Late June

Hogueras de San Juan (Alicante city): The most famous and popular of the city's fiestas, with effigies like those of the Valencian *fallas* (see above) burnt on St John's night after a week of all-night street parties and live music. The fiesta dates from the 1920s, but the tradition of fire festivals on summer solstice is pre-Christian. Midnight fireworks over the bay follow the *Nit del Foc*. Smaller *Hogueras* take place around the same time in Jávea, Denia, Benidorm, Calpe and Pego, and street bonfires in most villages.

July 15–16

Fiesta del Carmen (Tarbarca, San Pedro del Pinatar and other Mar Menor villages, Villajoyosa): The main fiesta of Spanish fishing ports. Images of the *Virgen del Carmen*, the fishermen's saint, are carried round the harbour and/or taken out to sea to bless the decked-out fleet. There are boat races, beach parties and fireworks.

'Hogueras' de San Juan

Mid-July

Santísima Sangre (Denia): The fiestas include a battle of flowers and, most famously, the *bous en la mar*, in which bulls are released in an arena on the quayside so that either they or their human persecutors fall into the sea.

August 14–15

Misterio de Elche: Elche's mystery play, comparable only to Oberammergau, tells of the Assumption of the Virgin Mary in a sung drama. It is the only European mystery play that has kept its medieval form (a 14th-century text) and is still performed in a church – the Basilica. The Basilica was designed around the play: during the play spectacular aerial machinery is lowered to the floor of the church from the dome. The performers are townspeople, and some parts are handed down through families. Tickets need to be booked well in advance from the Elche tourist office. A shortened version is also performed. In the final *Nit de l'Alba* the city explodes through the night in a stunning display of fireworks. But take care, there are invariably casualties.

Mid-August

Fiestas de la Vendimia (Jumilla): a week-long fiesta celebrating the grape harvest. The town fountain runs with wine and the first batch of grape juice out of the press is blessed.

September

Fiestas de Cartagineses y Romanos (Cartagena): along the lines of the *Moros y Cristianos* celebrated in the region but exclusive to Cartagena. It celebrates the expulsion of the Romans from the city. There is an elaborate wedding between Hanibal and Himilce and a meeting of the Roman senate.

Evening view through palms to Elche

Arts & Cultural Festivals

Mid-August

Certamen de Habaneras (Torrevieja): The rhythmic choral *habaneras* were brought to Spain by 19th-century sailors and exporters from Cuba. The festival consists of a week-long programme backed up by various other musical events. To get hold of tickets in advance, contact the town hall, tel: 96 571 2570.

Late August

Festival Nacional del Cante de las Minas (La Unión): Founded only in 1960, this festival preserves the dying art of the flamenco mining songs, which were introduced to the region in the nineteenth century by immigrant Andalucian mine workers.

Held every year in the wonderful Modernist market building, this festival is now ranked along with the most important flamenco events in Spain. Tickets can be bought in advance from tourist offices.

Early September

Festival de Folklore del Mediterráneo (Murcia): This festival highlights a different country each year, but there are always participating groups from all over the world.

Practical Information

GETTING THERE

By Air

Both British Airways and Iberia operate scheduled flights to the Costa Blanca. If you can be flexible about your departure date and time, you should be able to pick up a cheaper charter deal to Alicante; as a general rule, the longer you wait to buy your ticket, the cheaper it will be.

The region has three airports: El Altet (tel: 96 691 9000), 10km (6 miles) to the southwest of Alicante; Manises (tel: 96 370 9500), 15km (9 miles) west of Valencia; and San Javier (tel: 968 172 000), on the coast 40km (25 miles) to the southeast of Murcia.

Transport to and from Airports

Some international car-hire firms have branches at the airports where you can collect or hire a car.

A taxi ride from **El Altet airport** to the centre of Alicante takes 15 minutes. Buses run to and from town every twenty minutes between 7am and 9.20pm; the journey time is roughly 40 minutes. There is a bus between the airport and Elche about every two hours.

A bus runs between Valencia bus station and **Manises airport** at hourly intervals between about 6am and 9pm; allow 45 minutes for the trip.

From **San Javier airport**, you will need to get a taxi to San Javier town, then a bus to Murcia. The bus leaves once every two hours and the journey takes one hour.

By Boat

There are two direct car ferry routes from Britain to Spain. Brittany Ferries sails from Plymouth to Santander (tel: 0990 360 360) and P&O European ferries from Portsmouth to Bilbao (tel: 0990 980 555). Both crossings take over 24 hours. Weather conditions in the Bay of Biscay can be rough, and cancellations can occur, particularly in autumn and winter.

By Car

To drive from Britain to southeastern Spain will take at least two or three days or 30 hours minimum if you drive non-stop, even if you travel on the expensive French motorways. If you're driving from Santander to Alicante, you should allow 10–15 hours for the journey.

Your car must be equipped with a wing mirror on each side, headlamp

deflectors, a warning triangle and a set of spare light bulb. For peace of mind, consider taking out continental cover with a reputable breakdown service.

You will need a 'green card' (international insurance certificate), your log book and a Spanish bail bond. This document will prevent the Spanish police from locking you up if you injure somebody in an accident. It is advisable to carry an International Driving Permit or a Spanish translation of your driving license; some kind of licence must be carried at *all* times.

By Coach

Coach travel to the Costa Blanca is relatively cheap, but the journey – from London via the Channel ports and France, then down the Spanish coast past Valencia and on to Alicante and Murcia – takes an arduous 1½ days, so take a good book and sleeping pills or a bottle of whisky.

By Train

Tickets for journeys between Britain and Spain can be obtained from any leading travel agents or from Rail Europe (tel: 0990 848 848). Thomas Cook publishes a comprehensive European timetable, which is available from its branch offices.

TRAVEL ESSENTIALS

When to Go

The Costa Blanca, protected by mountain ranges, enjoys a mild Mediterranean climate with year-round sunshine, low rainfall and moderately-high humidity. July and August are uncomfortably hot, with temperatures reaching 35°C (95°F) on a regular basis. The coolest months of the year are January and February, when temperatures range from a low 7°C (44°F) to a pleasant 17°C (63°F). These also tend to be the wettest months of the year, along with March and April.

Thick, heavy clothes are unnecessary, even in winter. In summer, light clothes made from natural fibres are preferable, and sunglasses are essential if you are doing a lot of driving.

During the summer months many banks, department stores, high-class hotels, restaurants and public transport vehicles are air-conditioned. In winter some hotels and restaurants, particularly in the higher, cooler regions, are centrally heated.

The sea temperature is ideal for bathing from April to early November, although braver swimmers can be spotted taking a dip in winter.

January and February are the best months to see and smell the pink-and-white almond blossom. During the

spring months lemon and orange blossoms, and many other Mediterranean plants are in flower. If you are a bird-watcher, go in winter to see the spectacle of migrating flamingos at the saltpans and lakes along the coast south of Alicante.

Entry Requirements

British and other EU nationals, as well as nationals from the US, Australia and New Zealand need only a valid passport to enter Spain for a period of up to three months. Visitors from other countries should check with their nearest Spanish embassy.

What to wear

Spanish people tend to dress with a casual elegance, but it is perfectly acceptable to wear scruffy or beach clothes in tourist areas. For the sake of decorum, you should be well covered when visiting churches, monasteries, etc. Nor is it a good idea to explore inland areas in skimpy beach wear, as this may shock older people.

Electricity

Plugs have two round pins. Voltage is 220 AC. A converter and/or an adaptor plug may be useful if you want to take electrical appliances with you.

Time

Spain is one hour ahead of Greenwich Mean Time (GMT) in the winter, and two hours ahead in the summer. In January, the sun rises at about 8.15am and sets at about 6pm; the corresponding times in June

are 5.45am and 8.15pm, although the light lingers for another two hours.

Measurements

The metric system of measurement is used in Spain.

GETTING ACQUAINTED

Crowds

July and August are the peak months for tourists, both Spanish and foreign. This is a good time if you like lively coastal resorts, because some of them are rather lifeless out of season. However, if you are looking for a peaceful holiday and want to avoid inflated prices, you are advised to stay away from the coast during this period.

Fiestas

At all times of year you are sure to find a fiesta or an arts festival somewhere (see *Calendar of Special Events*). If you value your sleep, make your base outside the town and travel in for the festivities (but remember that roads in the centre are often closed to non-residents). Sight-seeing can be frustrating at fiesta time: it is hard to make your way around, and shops and museums may be closed.

Please note, too, that fiesta and festival tickets are usually available only direct from *ayuntamientos*.

Language

English is spoken by many people, as you would expect in a major tourist area. However, you will probably find a phrase book useful, and it is worth learning at least a few basic expressions before you go. A small effort on your part will help you to make friends with local people.

Attitudes to Tourists

British tourists do not have a very good reputation on the Costa Blanca as a result of the behaviour of *los hooligans*. However, the Spanish emphasise that the offenders are not only British, and are surprisingly helpful and friendly to foreigners, given the onslaught of the last 30 years.

Attitudes to Children

The Spanish dote on children, and they are sure to be given a warm welcome wherever they go; hotels are very understanding about their needs and will do their best to provide meals to suit.

You are unlikely to find a babysitter except by means of an informal personal arrangement, but it is part of the Spanish way of life for children to accompany adults to cafés, restaurants and fiestas, even very late at night.

Religion

Roman Catholicism is dominant throughout Spain, but only the Anglican and Evangelical denominations have Christian services in English (see local English-language press for details). There is a scattering of Jehovah's Witness churches throughout the area, as well as a synagogue in Benidorm and Buddhist temple in Benimantell.

Visiting churches can be tricky because, unless they are major landmarks, they are generally open only at the times of Mass, i.e. early morning and early evening, and all Sunday morning. At other times, or for smaller churches, you usually need to ask for the priest (*cura*), who may be available to give you the key and/or show you around. Monasteries and convents are open all day; ring the doorbell to be admitted.

Sex

There is a large divide in Spanish attitudes to sex: part of the population has become liberal since Franco's death, as a cursory glance at Spanish TV will confirm, while others remain dogmatically conservative. Legally, the minimum age for sex, both heterosexual and homosexual, between two consenting people is 18. All contraceptives are available at chemists, and condoms can be bought at supermarkets.

Harassment

Some women experience unwanted attention from local men. Historically, the Spanish have perceived foreign women as more likely than Spanish ones to be available for sex. On the whole, though, it is quite safe to travel alone, but if you are on the nervous side you may want to consider taking a personal alarm with you.

MONEY MATTERS

The peseta is the Spanish monetary unit. The coins are of 1, 5 (a *duro*), 10, 25, 50, 100, and 200 pesetas (ptas). There are notes of 500, 1,000, 2,000, 5,000 and 10,000 ptas.

Getting Cash

You can bring unlimited amounts of currency into Spain; you will need your passport to get hold of any more. Exchange rates are generally better for cash than for travellers' cheques and Eurocheques, and banks usually give you the best deal. A good exchange rate often means heavy commission, so shop around. If you change large sums of money at one time, you'll probably save on commission, but you'll have more to lose if you're mugged.

Many credit cards can be used to obtain cash. You can withdraw money over the counter during banking hours; if you know your Personal Identification Numbers (PIN), you will have access to cash from numerous 24-hour dispensers. If you use a credit card the exchange rate will be the one that is current when your cash advance is processed. There is no commission payable on credit-card advances, but you will have to pay a handling charge to the credit-card company; as interest is payable from the day the money is borrowed, this can turn out to be expensive.

Travellers' cheques are one of the safest ways of carrying money, as they can be replaced if necessary. There should be no trouble in using the major brands on the Costa Blanca.

Having money sent to Spain from abroad is complicated, expensive and time-consuming, and should be done in emergencies only. Contact your bank for further details.

Paying with Paper and Plastic

Many hotels, up-market restaurants and all department stores take credit cards, Visa and Mastercard being the most-widely accepted. You may have difficulty paying with Eurocheques in restaurants and shops, even in large or coastal towns. Travellers' cheques cannot usually be used to pay for goods.

GETTING AROUND

By Car

Remember to drive on the right and overtake on the left. This may sound elementary, but it is easy to forget on empty country roads.

Seat belts are compulsory. Speed limits are 60kph (38mph) in built-up areas, 100kph (62mph) on major roads, and 120kph (75mph) on motorways. Speeding fines are high and are payable on the spot. Children under 13 must sit in the back seat.

In large town or city centres, on-street parking spaces are hard to find, although expensive multi-storey car parks generally have room. Anarchic and double parking are national pastimes in Spain, but don't be fooled into thinking that the police never give parking tickets or tow cars away.

Petrol grades are super (97 octane), normal (92 octane), unleaded (95 octane) and diesel. Unleaded petrol is a couple of pesetas cheaper than leaded petrol, but you may have to hunt for it.

There are two kinds of motorway in Spain: *autopista* (which you must pay a toll to use) and *autovía* (which is free). An expensive toll is levied on the motorway north of Alicante (about 800ptas Alicante to Denia, for example); there is no charge south of Alicante and on the N330 past Elda and Villena. The motorway can be a good investment in summer and during the rest of the year in rush hours. These are generally linked to exoduses from towns at weekends and holidays, and influxes to town for highjinks at night and the return to work at the end of the weekends. The siesta period (approximately 3–5pm) is a good time to travel. Local roads to beaches are often congested on public holidays and Sundays in summer. Heavy roadworks between Alcoi and Xàtiva and between Murcia and Cartagena (for the building of the motorway) are likely for the foreseeable future.

An unnerving minority of Spanish drivers are impatient or love to take risks. Beware of those who ignore red traffic lights, pedestrian crossings, etc. In case of an accident, there are SOS points every 5kms (3 miles) on major roads; the police emergency phone number is 091. Make sure you obtain full details from any other driver involved. Any injury, however slight, has to be reported to the police, and the injured person must be taken to hospital.

Hiring a Car

A British travel agent should be able to arrange car hire for you, but small local companies are generally cheaper than big international ones. If you're under 23 and/or you have less than two years' driving experience, you'll probably find it difficult to rent a car.

You will need your passport and an International Driving Permit (your British licence will probably be accepted). All firms charge a set fee per day, plus IVA (tax) and insurance. Some firms charge extra for mileage. A hefty deposit is usually required unless you pay by credit card.

Hiring a Moped or Bicycle

Bicycles and mopeds for hire are easy to find in coastal resorts, and relatively cheap. To hire a moped, you must be aged 16 or over and have your passport and driving licence. Spanish moped riders rarely wear helmets, but they are compulsory and should be worn for safety reasons. Mopeds use *mezcla* (mixed) petrol.

Road and Walking Maps

The best map of the Iberian peninsula is the Michelin 1:1,000,000, No. 990. Michelin also publishes a 1:400,000 map, No. 445, which includes the Costa Blanca and has an index of place names.

A 1:200,000 and various 1:50,000 maps of the area can be obtained from the **Instituto Geografico Nacional** (IGN): Plaza de San Juan de Dios 3 (tel: 96 525 7312) in Murcia, and Avda. Frederico Soto 12 (tel: 968 521 3504) in Alicante. It is unlikely that you will find large-scale maps of the region, especially reliable ones, elsewhere.

By Taxi

Taxis are good for getting around towns and are generally cheaper than in Britain. An available taxi displays either a green light or a sign saying *libre*. The meter should be running. Surcharges are added to the basic fare at night (11pm to 6am), at weekends and on public holidays, and for trips outside the city. Tipping (5–10 percent of the fare) is expected.

By Coach

There is no single national coach line; ask at tourist offices where you need to go for your destination. Local coach services can only be booked and paid for in Spain, and seat reservations should be made in advance. Coach stations are laid out according to the company, not the route.

By Train

Tickets can be bought at train stations, RENFE (the Spanish railway network) travel offices or any authorised travel agency at any time between 60 days and five minutes before departure. There are different types of train, varying in price and speed from the fast *talgo* down to the slow *exprés*.

Discount fares are available on off-peak days (*días azules*). On production of suitable identification, senior citizens, families with children and young people under 26 can also obtain discounts off the normal price. You can buy a tourist pass valid for unlimited travel within Spain for periods of 8, 15 or 22 days. A rail guide including fares (issued monthly) can be obtained at any Spanish train station. The relevant RENFE routes within this area are Cartagena–Alicante–Valencia, Alicante–Madrid, and Cartagena–Murcia–Albacete–Madrid. For further information, tel: 96 592 0202, bookings, tel: 96 522 9169.

The Costa Blanca Express (*also see the itinerary Pick & Mix 6, page 61*), operated by FGV on a narrow-gauge railway, leaves Alicante every hour. All trains travel as far as Benidorm, and about half complete the two-hour journey to Denia.

In summer months, the train also runs a night service, the Trensnochador, serving the resorts and returning from Denia in the early hours of the morning. The Lemon Express uses the same line, and runs from Benidorm to Gata and back once a day (with visits). Reservations can be made at Benidorm station, tel: 96 585 1895.

By Sea

You can find out about or book the following ferry services through any local travel agency.

Hydrofoil to Ibiza: Flebasa, tel: 902 160 180, runs daily hydrofoil services from Denia to Ibiza; the journey takes about three hours.

Ferries to the Balearic Islands: Trasmediterranea, tel: 902 454 645, has regular sailings from the port of Valencia to Mallorca, Menorca and Ibiza.

Ferry to Tabarca: The shortest journey is via Santa Pola (25 minutes); this route and the one from Alicante are both operated by Kontiki, tel: 521 6396, from April to November. The longest route, between Torrevieja and Tabarca, takes one and half hours and runs daily from June to September. For tickets and further information, tel: 670 2122.

HOURS AND HOLIDAYS

Business Hours

Shops are generally open from 9am–1pm and 4–8pm Monday–Saturday; in resort towns many stay open on Sundays.

Post offices are open from 9am–2pm Monday–Friday, and from 9am–1pm on Saturday.

Banks operate Monday– Friday from 8.30am or 9am to 2 pm; some branches stay open on Saturday, but close an hour earlier. They are closed on Sunday and all official holidays. Outside banking hours, you may be able to change money at a hotel, station, airport or department store.

Public Holidays

The following dates are public holidays in the Costa Blanca region: January 1 and 6, March 19, Easter Thursday, Good Friday, May 1, August 15, October 9 and 12, November 1, December 6, 8 and 25. Local holidays are in late June (San Juan), on the Monday of Easter week and on Thursday after Easter (Santa Faz).

If you are planning to travel to the Costa Blanca over the Christmas or Easter periods, do not worry about finding everything shut down for weeks – this is not the case.

WHERE TO STAY

Hotels

Hotels are graded from one to five stars, *hostales* from one to three and *pensiones* from one to two. The appropriate category is displayed on a blue plaque at the entrance. If you are looking for atmosphere, you can't beat the state-run chain of *paradores*. These luxury hotels are often in renovated convents or castles or, like the one in Xàbia (Jávea), modern buildings in privileged settings. At the other end of the market there are increasing numbers of bed and breakfasts (*casas rurales*) appearing in the countryside away from the coast.

All hotels are required to display prices (including service and tax) at the reception desk and in every bedroom, and to have a complaints book (*Hoja Oficial de Reclamaciones*) for customers' use. Any complaint must be sent to the relevant authorities within 48 hours, so a request to use the book will probably solve any argument.

Hotels will usually do your laundry if requested. You'll be lucky to find a self-service launderette outside coastal resorts.

Tourist offices can provide you with details of adequate but uninspiring hotels, of all categories and price ranges, on the Costa Blanca. The following list is a personal selection of hotels that have character, are in pleasant locations and are a little different form the run-of-the-mill establishments. They are all popular so its best to book ahead (especially for the summer and weekends in coastal towns, for winter and weekdays in inland towns). Most have staff who like to practise their English.

Prices given are for accommodation only, in a double room with bathroom, during the high season.

In Towns

Alicante/Alacant: Hotel Palas (three stars), Pl. de Mar 2, tel: 96 520 9310. Grand and shabbily elegant, with décor reminiscent of bygone days. Garage. 10,000ptas.
Altea: Hostal Fornet (no stars), C. Beniardá 1, tel: 96 584 3005. Some rooms have a terrace and views of the sea and Cathedral. Garage for extra 500ptas. 5,500ptas.
Cartagena: Los Habaneros, San Diego 60, tel: 968 505 250. A modest and functional hotel with rooms at reasonable prices. 7,400ptas.
La Manga del Mar Menor: Príncipe Felipe, Los Belones, tel: 968 331 234. The hotel is part of the luxurious complex La Manga Club, built in the style of a Spanish village. Among its many facilities are golf courses, swimming pools, tennis courts and a health centre. 44,800ptas.
Denia: Las Rotas (two stars), Partida Las Rotas 71, tel: 96 578 0323. By the sea just outside Denia. Tennis court, and restaurant leading out to pool (April–October). Parking. 10,500ptas.
Elche/Elx: Hotel Huerto del Cura (four stars), Porta de la Morera 14, tel: 96 545 8040. Modern *parador* in the palm forest, including individual chalets in an attractive garden. Swimming pool and tennis court; garage. 16,500ptas.
Lorca: Hostal del Carmen (one star). C. Rincón de los Valientes 3, tel: 968 466 459. Among the very few places to stay. Small, clean *pensión* in the centre of town. Good local cooking; on-street parking. 5,500ptas.
Murcia: Hotel Arco de San Juan (four stars), Pl. de Ceballos 10, tel: 968 210 455. Built on the site of an 18th-century palace and retaining the original facade. Unusual décor and many works of art; parking. 17,500ptas.
Villajoyosa: El Montiboli, Partida Montiboli s/n, La Vila Joiosa, tel: 96 589 0250. A seaside hotel perched on a low cliff outside the small resort of Villajoyosa, south of Benidorm. 30,250ptas.
Xàbia/Jávea: Parador de la Costa Blanca (four stars), Playa del Arenal 2, tel: 96 579 0200. Uninspiring architecture, but privileged position on the seafront. Swimming pool and garden; garage. 18,500ptas.

Off the Beaten Track.

Agres: Pensión Mariola (no stars), C. San Antonio 4, on road into village, tel: 96 551 0017. Plain, almost spartan rooms, comfortable lounge and huge, rustic dining room; parking. 3,300ptas.
Balneario de Archena: Hotel Termas (four stars), Carr. Balneario s/n, tel: 968 670 100. Access via stairs and tunnels to baths and fountains below. Covered parking. 10,500ptas.
Caravaca de la Cruz: Hostal-Restaurante Caballos del Vino, Carr. Murcia 71 (two stars), tel: 968 702 219. On main road into Caravaca from Cehegin. Serves excellent food around the clock. Parking. 4,500ptas.
Confrides: El Pirineo (no stars), C. San Antonio 52, tel; 96 588 5858. Good base for exploring Costa Blanca; inland but within easy reach of the coast. Homely family-run hotel, local cooking; parking. 5,500ptas with breakfast.
Moratalla: Hostal Levante (no stars), Carr. del Canal 21, no telephone. Outside the village centre. Family-run bar-restaurant with rooms upstairs. Parking. 3,000ptas.
Tabarca: Casa Gobernador (2 stars). Wonderful hotel on an island, inside a historic building, with local cooking. 9,000ptas.

Ferry to Tabarca

Renting a Villa

Self-catering accommodation is not usually rented for less than a week at a time, and usually in calendar monthly or fortnightly blocks. Advertisements in British national newspapers and specialist magazines are the best sources for finding a villa. More characterful local houses can be tracked down by travelling around yourself, or phoning the newly established central reservations office, Noratur, tel: 968 706 600.

Camping and Caravanning

Most campsites are concentrated along the coast, and only the official sites are legal. They are classified according to prices and amenities: luxury, then first to third class. Most sites have running water and electricity. Prices, which at the more luxurious sites are similar to those of a cheap hotel, must be displayed at each entrance.

At many sites it is possible to camp all year round, although outside the peak summer months there may be fewer amenities and the site may have an out-of-season feel.

Although none of the campsites on the Costa Blanca itself is for people who like to get back to nature, the following is a small selection of those with something to set them apart from the masses. All the sites listed are open throughout the year.

Benidorm: Caravanning-Camping Villasol (first class), Camino Viejo de Valencia s/n, tel: 96 585 0422. The most central and most luxurious. Outdoor and indoor swimming pools. **Elche/Elx**: Camping El Palmeral, C. Curtidores s/n, tel: 968 542 2766. Luxury.

In the middle of the palm forest. Swimming pool.

Moratalla: La Puerta (second class), tel: 968 730 008. Beautifully situated model campsite in forest in river valley with waterfall. Swimming pool, tennis court, barbecues, spring water. Nearby Bullas also has a good site.

HEALTH & EMERGENCIES

If you are not used to strong sun you should take appropriate precautions. In summer, sightseeing is best done in the early morning or late afternoon, when the heat is more bearable than it is in the middle of the day. The Spanish don't have a midday siesta for nothing!

Eating and Drinking

Not all tap water on the Costa Blanca is drinkable, and none of it has a particularly pleasant taste. Bottled mineral water, sparkling (*con gas*) or still (*sin gas*), is readily available in shops and restaurants.

Excessive amounts of alcohol or cold drinks during hot weather are a common cause of 'Spanish tummy'. Fruit and vegetables should always be washed carefully. If you are caught short, don't hesitate to use the toilets in a bar or petrol station; this is common practice because there aren't many public toilets elsewhere.

Chemists

A green or red cross sign identifies a chemist (*farmacia*). They are generally open from 9.30am–2pm and from 4pm–8pm on weekdays, and for the morning hours only on Saturday. Outside these times, a list of on-duty chemists providing an emergency service can be found in the local newspaper or posted on the door of each pharmacy.

Spanish pharmacists are highly trained paramedics, and can deal with many minor ailments. You can freely buy some medicines, including certain antibiotics, that in Britain are available only on prescription.

You can get a large discount on the cost of medicines if you have a Spanish doctor's prescription; you may find it difficult to use a foreign prescription in Spain.

National Health Services

If you are an EU resident and have an E111 form (obtainable from the Dept. of Social Security) you are eligible for free treatment from the Spanish national health service. For extra protection, take out medical insurance as well. Vaccinations are not needed for visitors from Britain.

If your case is urgent, ask a chemist or your hotel for directions to a public hospital (*residencia* or *hospital*); take the original and a photocopy of your E111 form if you have one; if not, take your passport along instead.

Facilities for the Disabled

Although awareness of the needs of disabled people is increasing, facilities, such as lifts and adapted toilets are still few and far between.

Crime & Emergencies

Take elementary precautions to avoid being the victim of crime. In coastal resorts and big towns, beware of pickpockets, con artists and bag snatchers. Don't sit in your car with your bag or purse on your lap; it may be snatched by thieves on a motorbike. Don't leave valuables in your car or in your hotel room, and watch your possessions carefully if you are on the beach. Shoulder

bags should be slung across the body, not left to hang loosely.

Away from towns, there is little problem. If anything is stolen, go to the local police station; the police are unlikely to try to find your belongings, but you will need to fill in a form for insurance purposes.

While wandering around old quarters, you may be approached by drug dealers. Drug dealing and trafficking are illegal in Spain.

In an emergency, British citizens should contact the **British Consulate** in Alicante (Pl. Calvo Sotelo 1, tel: 96 521 6190). US citizens should contact the **US Embassy** in Madrid (Calle Serrano, 75; tel: 91 587 2200).

COMMUNICATIONS & MEDIA

Post

Letters can be weighed and stamps purchased at a tobacconist (*estanco*) as well as at post offices. Airmail to Britain takes two to ten days to arrive – less if you pay an extra charge to send it *urgente*, and you put it in a red postbox (standard letters go in yellow ones).

Letters can be sent to you in Spain

c/o main post offices.
Sender writes:

Your name,
Lista de Correos,
Place name,
Province name,
Spain.

You will need proof of identity to collect correspondence.

Telegrams, Telex and Faxes

Telegrams and telexes may be sent via any post office. You can also phone a telegram from anywhere in the region by dialling 2222000, prefixed by the area code (96 in Alicante and Valencia provinces, 968 in Murcia province). You are likely to be able to fax from a printer, copy shop or stationer (*papelería*).

Telephones

Public phone boxes have instructions for use in English. There are also large telephone offices where calls are paid for after they have been made; you can make a reverse-charge call (*cobro revertido*) from these offices or from a call box. Many bars, hotels, restaurants and petrol stations have coin-operated phones. For Spanish directory enquiries dial 1003; for international enquiries dial 025.

To call other countries first dial the international access code 07, then the relevant country code: Australia (61); France (33); Germany (49); Italy (39); Japan (81); Netherlands (31); UK (44); US and Canada (1).

If you are using a US credit phone card, dial the company's access number below, then 01, and then the country code. Sprint tel: 900 99 0013; AT&T tel: 900 99 0011; MCI tel: 900 99 0014. The international code for Spain is 34; the area code for Alicante and Valencia provinces is 96 and for Murcia province 968. You need to use this area code at all times even if you are phoning within a province or indeed within a small town.

Newspapers

National newspapers you might find interesting include *El País* (centre-left), *Diario 16* and *ABC* (centre-right) and *El Mundo* (unclear). The *Costa Blanca News* and the *Entertainer* are published in English and are targeted primarily at expatriate residents, as is the glossy magazine *Lookout*, which can be a good source of background reading on Spain. They are available mostly in coastal resorts, where the international press can also be bought a day after publication.

Events Listings

These can be found in all of the publications mentioned above. Town halls and tourist offices in large towns often publicise events with large poster or a what's on list.

English-Language Books

Don't expect to find anything other than popular fiction paperbacks on sale. Most large bookshops sell at least some English-language books: the best in Alicante is Ochenta Mundos (Avda. General Marvá). There are English-language bookshops dotted along the coast, at Alfaz del Pi, Benidorm, Calpe, Denia, Xàbia (Jávea) and Torrevieja, where international newspapers are also available.

TV and Radio

There are two national public television channels in Spanish (Castilian): TVE1 and TVE2. There are also two private channels (Antenna 3 and Tele 5), and the subscription-only Canal +. International satellite channels, including many English-language ones, are widely available in hotels and bars. The Costa Blanca area also receives the regional television channel Canal 9, in Valencian, and TVE3, in Catalan.

The BBC World Service can generally be picked up on a short-wave radio. The recommended frequencies for this area are 15.070MHz/19.19m and 12.095MHz/24.80m.

Some local radio stations have a small part of their output in English: you can check the local English-language press for details.

USEFUL ADDRESSES

Tourist Information Offices

This guide book is necessarily selective in its coverage. You can obtain a wealth of further information from tourist offices. Even if you are somewhere which doesn't have a tourist office, the town hall may be able to help (for example in Alcoi, Biar, Caravaca de la Cruz, Monóvar or Yecla).

Opening hours vary, and fluctuate considerably. Most offices are open for approximately four hours in the morning and another three hours in the late afternoon. Many are open on Saturday morning. During the summer months some are open longer, and large towns often set up temporary summer offices in addition to the all-year-round ones. However, most are closed on Sunday throughout the year.

Alicante/Alacant: Explanada de España 2, on the seafront, tel: 96 520 0000; Pl. de Ayuntamiento, at the town hall, tel: 96 514 9251; C. Portugal 17, by the coach station, tel: 96 592 9802; Alicante Airport, tel: 96 691 9367.

Altea: C. St Pierre 9, tel: 96 584 4114.
Benidorm: Avda. Martínez Alejos 16, in the old town near the town hall, tel: 96 585 3224.
Calpe/Calp: Avda. Ejércitos Españoles 66, between the seafront and the old town, tel: 96 583 1250.
Cartagena: Pl. del Ayuntamiento s/n, at the town hall by the port, tel: 96 850 6483.
Denia: Plaza Oculista Buigues 9, tel: 96 642 2367.
Elche/Elx: Paseo de la Estacíon s/n, located in the municipal park, tel: 96 545 2747.
Gandía: C. Marques de Campo s/n, in front of train station, tel: 96 284 2407.
Lorca: C. Lopes Gisbert s/n, near the San Mateo church, tel: 968 466 157.
Los Alcázares: Avda de la Libertad 50, in the town hall, tel: 171 361.
Murcia: C. San Cristobál 6, tel: 968 366 100, 366 130.
Orihuela/Oriola: C. Francisco Díez 25, near the town hall, tel: 96 530 2747.
Santa Pola: Pl. de la Diputacíon 6, situated in the palm gardens, tel: 96 699 2276.
Torrevieja: Plaza Ruíz Capdepont s/n, tel: 96 571 5936.
Xàbia/Jávea: Pl. del Almirante Bastarreche 24, by the port, tel: 96 579 0736.

Xàtiva/Játiva: C. Noguera 10, near the Cathedral, tel: 96 227 3346.

In England: 22–23 Manchester Square, London W1M 5AP, tel: 0171 486 8077 (9.15am–4.15pm Monday– Friday). It is best to visit in person or to write, as the phone can be engaged for a lot of the time.

FURTHER READING

There are very few other guide books or travel accounts that deal with this region in isolation. However, the books recommended below will give you a good insight into Spain's character. They can be consulted at public libraries and the following institutions:

Canning House, 2 Belgrave Square, London SW1.
Instituto Cervantes, 102 Eaton Square, London SW1.

Books

Brenan, Gerald. *The Face of Spain*. Penguin, 1988 (first published in 1950).
Hooper, John. *The Spaniards*. Penguin, 1987.
Hooper, John. *The New Spaniards*. Penguin, 1994.
Macaulay, Rose. *The Fabled Shore*. Oxford University Press, 1986.
Pritchett, V S. *The Spanish Temper*. Hogarth, 1984.

ART/PHOTO CREDITS

Photography **Roger Mort *and***
page 85 **F Lisa Beebe**
page 106 **Roger Hilton**
page 110 **Annabel Elston / APA**

Design Concept **V Barl**
Cover Design **Klaus Geisler**
Cartography **Berndtson & Berndtson**

Index

A

B

C

D, E

F, G

H, I

J,K

L

M

N, O

P

Q, R

S

T

V

W, X, Y